SIR FREDERIC MADDEN

GARLAND REFERENCE LIBRARY
OF THE HUMANITIES
(VOL. 126)

SIR FREDERIC MADDEN
A Biographical Sketch and Bibliography

Robert W. Ackerman
Gretchen P. Ackerman

GARLAND PUBLISHING, INC. • NEW YORK & LONDON
1979

Library of Congress Cataloging in Publication Data

Ackerman, Robert William, 1910–
  Sir Frederic Madden : a biographical sketch and
bibliography.

  (Garland reference library of the humanities ; 126)
  Includes index.
  1. Madden, Frederic, Sir, 1801–1873.   2. Madden,
Frederic, Sir, 1801–1873—Bibliography.   3. Philologists—
England—Biography.   4. Medievalists—England—
Biography.   5. British Museum. Dept. of Manuscripts—
Biography.   I. Ackerman, Gretchen P., joint author.
PE64.M25A62   016.41'092'4   78-68237
ISBN 0-8240-9819-6

Printed on acid-free, 250-year-life paper
Manufactured in the United States of America

CONTENTS

ACKNOWLEDGMENTS

In the process of preparing the present bibliography and life sketch of Frederic Madden, we have drawn on the special competence of many students of medieval literature and history, and we have taxed the patience of many librarians. For their unstinting cooperation, we are most grateful, although responsibility for errors and omissions in our work must naturally be laid at our door alone.

It was ten years ago in the Bodleian Library that we first innocently called for the Madden Diary, only in due course to be confronted by forty-three sizeable volumes filling an entire library truck. Correctly reading our expressions, the Keeper of Western Manuscripts, Dr. R.W. Hunt, quietly came forward to advise us that a microfilm copy of the whole Diary would soon be obtainable. Our initial intention had been only to determine whether by chance Madden had jotted down in his journal any interesting entries relating to two of his well-known editions of Middle English romances. But a sampling of his astounding life record led imperceptibly into a rapt and systematic reading of the whole, and we were then lost, an experience, as we learned subsequently, shared by others. Thus, to Dr. Hunt, from whom we received permission to quote from the Diary and other Madden material, we owe a considerable debt. With manuscript material other than the Diary, we have more recently been generously assisted by Mr. Timothy Rogers, also of the Bodleian Library.

In the formulation and during all later stages of our project, Mr. M.A.F. Borrie, Assistant Keeper of Manuscripts at the British Library, has been of indispensable help. Not only did he call to our attention newly acquired and not yet catalogued Madden documents while we were working in his department, but he has painstakingly responded to tedious questions about bibliographical minutiae and mailed to us photocopies of Madden's juvenilia. As noted again in the introduction, Mr. Borrie and Mr. Alan Bell of the National Library of Scotland are planning a collaborative edition of the Diary, and both have published useful papers on the subject. The Under-Librarian of the Cambridge University Library, B. Jenkins, has been similarly kind in answering queries about manuscript material.

We wish further to thank librarians at the Houghton Library at Harvard University and the Beinecke Library at Yale University, in which some manuscripts and annotated books are preserved. Again, we were made to feel at home during many visits to the Baker Library, Dartmouth College, where we carried out our final check of nineteenth-century periodicals.

Encouragement of primary importance has been forthcoming from Professor A.S.G. Edwards of the University of Victoria, who has himself written about Madden and who, in fact, first broached the possibility of the present book to us. He has, moreover, supplied us with a number of titles which we might otherwise have missed in compiling our bibliography. Reassuring interest has been expressed by fellow medievalists, prominent among whom are Professors Fred C. Robinson of Yale University and Roy F. Leslie of the University of Victoria. The latter is currently occupied, along with G.L. Brook, with the third and final volume of an edition of Layamon's *Brut*, the *editio princeps* of which was published by Madden just over a century ago.

We are deeply appreciative as well for travel grants and a study grant from the American Council of Learned Societies and the American Philosophical Society that enabled us to pursue our work in England in 1968, 1969, 1972, and 1975.

R.W.A.
G.P.A.

INTRODUCTION

As the editor of a number of major works of medieval literature and history and also of the Wycliffite Bible, Sir Frederic Madden (FM) has been well known and highly respected by generations of students of the Middle Ages. He possessed a prodigious fund of precise learning and, in his impeccable presentation of Middle English and Latin texts, he may fairly be said to have set the canons of what we regard today as responsible editorial scholarship.

In view of such achievements and also of his many fruitful years as Keeper of Manuscripts in the British Museum, now the British Library, it is strange that no systematic effort has heretofore been made to compile a bibliography of his numerous works. Even the obituary notices of 1873 offer only a meager impression of the range of his scholarly enterprises. Nor has he been made the subject of a separate biography, a surprising omission when one takes into account his immense and uninhibited Diary deposited in the Bodleian Library, Oxford, and thrown open to the public in 1920. It is true that Arundell Esdaile's *British Museum Library* and two more recent histories by Edward Miller (see Bibliography C) provide, although in disconnected form, much information about FM's thirty-nine years in the Department of Manuscripts. The experience of both these writers as keepers and administrators in the Museum and their resulting familiarity with relevant Parliamentary papers, minutes of Trustees' meetings, and similar archival material enable them to assess FM's discharge of his official responsibilities with authority. In the 1950's, T.C. Skeat of the Department of Manuscripts took note of such of FM's services to the Museum as his thoroughgoing rearrangement and correction of Ayscough's catalogue of 1782, in which task Lady Madden proved to be a valuable assistant.

Of the above-mentioned writers, Miller in particular makes effective use of FM's Diary and correspondence as well as the memoirs and papers of other figures of the day. The same is decidedly true of authors of several studies concerned only indirectly with FM, notably A.N.L. Munby, C.K. Francis Brown, A.S.G. Edwards, Mrs. J.E. Graham, and D.A. Winstanley. Understandably, none of them deals with FM as a scholar or seeks to depict the whole person revealed in the Diary and other records: one of the most interesting and, within limitations, intellectually vigorous men of the middle decades of the nineteenth century. For in addition to chronicling his almost obsessive literary labors, his involvement in philological disputes, and his detecting and unmasking of some of the most impudent manuscript thieves and forgers of any age, FM brings us into intimate contact with the raw emotions generated by his personal and professional problems and the details of his rôle in the day-to-day life of his times.

A major aim of the present book is to make available a list as nearly complete as possible of FM's published writings, virtually all of them on literary, historical, and antiquarian subjects (Bibliography A). These are set down in chronological order according to date of appearance and are numbered as well for ready reference. Many of the titles are annotated with references to pertinent Diary entries, reviews, and the like. The short Supplement to Bibliography A lists representative manuscript catalogues drawn up by FM or prepared under his supervision.

Bibliography B consists largely of unpublished matter, some of it in FM's handwriting, and also FM's "special collections" of ballads and newspaper clippings and pictures of historical interest. Several categories are distinguished: I. Life Records, including Correspondence; II. Working Papers, including Annotated Books; and III. Special Collections and Miscellanea.

The third list, Bibliography C, consists of publications concerned with FM and also selected treatments of the British Museum Library in the nineteenth century, the lives of a few of FM's friends and associates, and relevant aspects of social history. Official records bearing on FM's conduct of his duties are not included, but such documents, including minutes of the

Museum Trustees' meetings, Parliamentary papers, and the like, are set down under "Primary Sources" in Edward Miller's fine history of the Museum (Bib. No. 287).

To acquire an adequate knowledge of FM's writings without a close preliminary study of the Diary and also the correspondence would scarcely be possible, for only therein may one learn about numerous of his shorter articles and notes. Many of these contributions were either published anonymously or signed, as was still the custom in those days, with fanciful *noms de plume* or with initials, themselves sometimes misleading. Pseudonyms and initials that may be shown on sufficient evidence to represent FM are listed and, when possible, explained in the table of abbreviations. We could, of course, have overlooked a few unsigned items that FM did not see fit to mention in the Diary or a letter. It is less likely that we have erred in ascribing to him works actually by the hands of others.

Preceding our bibliography is an essay, "Sir Frederic Madden: A Biographical Sketch," based on the Diary, correspondence, other autograph material, and also a high proportion of the works listed in Bibliography C. Apart from occasional parenthetical references, the life sketch is undocumented.

A true critical biography would naturally include, as ours does not, a close account and evaluation of FM as a librarian and administrative officer in a great national institution during a crucial stage of its development. But, as has already been stated, we are fortunate that thoroughly well-qualified historians, such as Esdaile and Miller, have given careful attention to FM's career in the Museum, not overlooking those personality traits that were largely responsible for his years of conflict with various colleagues, especially Panizzi, and which undoubtedly were important in his failure to achieve the dignity of Principal Librarian. In another respect as well, the present essay does not meet the expectations of a full biography: that is, we have not sought out living descendants of the Madden family or of families at one time or another acquainted with FM in the quest for letters or papers, such as the minute financial record and diary said by FM to have been maintained by his brother Henry.

As it stands, our short and severely factual life is meant only to provide a context for FM's publications, major and minor, and also for the unpublished revelations that flowed from his pen over a period in excess of fifty years. An appreciation of his always solid and sometimes brilliant contributions to our grasp of medieval literature and history may well be enhanced by some acquaintance with FM as a passionate medievalist, a learned curator of manuscripts, a great palaeographer and editor, and also a strong, very human individual.

It will be noted that FM's given name is here spelled "Frederic," the form he came to prefer over "Frederick." In 1855, when called upon to make a legal deposition as to his name, he stated that he had not used the "k" spelling since 1828, "but I cannot get other people to do the same" (D, 31 Mar. 1855). This is one of FM's rare inaccuracies, for he consistently subscribed himself as "Frederick" in publications through 1832, as on the title page of his *William and the Werwolf* appearing in that year. Also, his infant son by his first wife was hastily christened "Frederick" just before he followed his unfortunate young mother in death in February 1830. Only after 1832, in fact, does the "c" spelling become standard.

ABBREVIATIONS
including *Noms de Plume*

[Titles of periodicals are abbreviated only when referred to several times in the bibliography.]

AJ	*Archaeological Journal*
Arch.	*Archaeologia*
A.S.	See S.A. below.
Ath.	*Athenaeum*
Bib.	Bibliography
BL	British Library; in FM's day, and until recently, the British Museum (Library)
BM	British Museum (Library)
Bod.	Bodleian Library, Oxford University
"Bucca"	"Trumpeter"; term connected with a boys' game once used by FM in signing a note on the game
Camb.	Cambridge University Library
"Clerk of Oxenforde"	Pseudonym used once by FM
C.N.	Used occasionally by FM in signing articles. Final letters in Frederi(c) Madde(n). See K.N. below.
Corr.	Corresponding, as in Corresponding Member
CTG	*Collectanea Topographica et Genealogica*
D	FM's Diary. Bod. MS. hist. C. 140–82

EETS	*Early English Text Society (Original Series). EETS, ES, Early English Text Society (Extra Series)*
F.A.S.	See S.A. below.
FM, F.M.	Frederic Madden. "F.M." often used as a signature to articles
fol., fols.	folio, folios
F.R.S.(L.)	See R.S.(L.) below. "F.R.S." used once as the signature to an article
F.S.A.E.	Fellow of the Society of Antiquaries of Edinburgh
Gent. Mag.	*Gentleman's Magazine*
"Hantoniensis"	Used once as the signature to an article on Hamptonshire
Harv.	Houghton Library, Harvard University
K.C.B.	Knight Commander of the Bath
K.H.	Knight of the Guelphic Order of Hanover
K.N.	Used occasionally by FM in signing early articles. Final letters of Frederic(k) Madde(n)
M.	Frequently used by FM as a signature
μ	Lower case "mu," used infrequently by FM as a signature
M.M.	Used by FM in signing his epitaph to his cat
M. & N.	Used as the signature to one article, these letters seem to signify two authors, of which FM is the first
M.R.I.A.	Member of the Royal Irish Academy
M.R.S.L.	See R.S.(L.).

MS., MSS.	Manuscript, manuscripts
"Nauticus"	Used once by FM in signing an article dealing with the navy
N&Q	*Notes and Queries*
O.B.	Used once by FM as a signature. Possibly intended as an allusion to the Order of the Bath, a distinction held by FM's uncle
"Philagoras"	"Lover of the market place." Used once by FM in signing an article on the history of market fairs
PPGLSR	*The Portsmouth, Portsea, and Gosport Literary and Scientific Register*. Published by D.B. Price, 1822–23
P. & M.	Signature appended to an article in several parts in *CTG* evidently indicating that FM wrote the contribution with a collaborator, possibly Sir Francis Palgrave or Sir Thomas Phillipps
"Ritsonianus"	Used once by FM in signing an article concerned with Joseph Ritson
rpr.	Reprinted, reprint
R.S.(L.)	Royal Society of Literature of the United Kingdom. F.R.S.(L.), Fellow of the Royal Society; M.R.S.(L.), Member of the Royal Society
S.A.	Society of Antiquaries of London. F.S.A., Fellow of the Society of Antiquaries
S.C.	*A Summary Catalogue of the Western Manuscripts in the Bodleian Library at Oxford*, 7 vols. in 8, Oxford: Clarendon Press, 1895–1953
"Scrutator"	Used once in signing an article in the *Times*

Yale	Beinecke Library, Yale University
Z.	Used by FM in signing two of his earliest publications (Bib. Nos. 1 and 4), this initial may have been whimsically intended to suggest an exotic place of origin for the author. In yet another article in the same periodical as these two papers (Bib. No. 3), FM refers to "Zembla" as a notably remote location. Here, Zembla is apparently a corruption of Russian Novaya Zemlya ("new land"), an archipelago extending into the Arctic Ocean from the coast of European Russia. FM could well have borrowed this form from Alexander Pope, who several times alludes to "Zembla." For example, in his *Essay on Man* (epist. II, 24) occurs the line, "At Greenland, Zembla, or the Lord knows where" [Twickenham ed., Vol. III, ed. Maynard Mack (London and New Haven, 1964), 82]. See also Pope's "The Temple of Fame" [*ed. cit.*, Vol. II, ed. Geoffrey Tillotson (1954), 256, and the note on Zembla, 410–11].
*	Indicates publications making significant use of FM's Diary or correspondence
[. . .]	Indicates title supplied to periodical articles published without a title

PART ONE

SIR FREDERIC MADDEN

A BIOGRAPHICAL SKETCH

Frederic Madden was born in Portsmouth 16 February 1801 to
Captain of the Royal Marines William John Madden (1757-1833)
and Sarah Carter Madden (1759-1833). Frederic was the sev-
enth of the eight children who lived into adulthood and the
youngest of the four sons.
    His mother was the daughter of the Rev. Arnold Carter,
M.A., minor canon of Rochester Cathedral. His father was the
older of the two sons of James Madden, Esq. (died 1812), who
had left Ireland in 1747 and bought an estate, Cole Hill
House, at Fulham. The two sons sustained their perception of
themselves as gentry by entering the officer corps of the
armed services. Captain William John apparently did not en-
joy a distinguished military career and retired on half pay
long before his death. The prize family exhibit was the
younger brother, Major General Sir George Allen Madden (1771-
1828), Knight Commander of the Bath and Knight of the Portuguese Order of the Tower and Sword and of the Turkish Cres-
cent. After a gallant but turbulent early period of service
in Corsica and Egypt, George Allen was court-martialed for
insubordination and required to sell his commissions. In
1809, however, he was given high rank in the Portuguese for-
ces then operating with the allies against the French in the
Peninsular War. His great feat was leading a cavalry charge
at Fuente de Cantos, 15 September 1810, which was credited
with saving the Spanish army. Not long thereafter, he was
reinstated in the British army, advanced to the rank of major general, and awarded a K.C.B. He fought a bloodless duel
with an officer whose accusations, as he thought, had led to
his court-martial. Although never married, he was involved
in his middle years in several liaisons, as his nephew Frederic noted admiringly in going over his papers (D, 14 Dec.
1851). Sir George retained the family estate at Fulham but
died at his brother's house in Portsmouth, at age fifty-

seven. The family cherished the memory of his military funeral in the Portsmouth Garrison Church and erected a tablet
there in his honor.

     Given such a tradition, it is not surprising that FM's
brothers, Charles and Lewis, became Royal Navy and Marine officers respectively whereas the third brother, Henry, held a
post as a civilian in the War Office, his sister Clarissa
became the wife of Admiral Samuel Jackson, and their son
Keats was an army major. Moreover, of FM's own children,
George was in military service during his short and unfortunate life, and Emily Mary married Lieutenant Colonel Edward
Tedlie of the 60th Royal Rifles and spent a tour of duty with
him in India. After the Colonel's death in 1877, Emily Mary
became the wife of an early suitor, William Holley, and was
a second time left a widow in 1898. It was she who gave the
British Library the rather youthful portrait of her father
now hanging in the reading room of the Department of Manuscripts.

     Ostensibly, little in the life led by children of garrison
officers at Portsmouth could have encouraged intellectual
pursuits. FM's accounts of his last years in his father's
house are full of descriptions of military balls, attendance
at parades and receptions honoring the Regent or other dignitaries, of family and neighborhood gatherings, and of theater parties. At the age of eighteen, he was excited by a
close view of the Prince of Wales and a flattering conversation with the Duke of Clarence who, as William IV, was to
confer a knighthood on him fourteen years later. He congra-
tulated himself on his dancing, whether the quadrille or the
saraband, and it was at an assembly in the Green Row Rooms
that he met and danced with Mary Hayton, who became his first
wife. He was equally vain about his skill at chess, and he
recorded carefully his victories over friends and local
champions, many of them military men. He also found time for
an occasional fling with girls of the lower classes, and some
of these escapades he memorialized in cypher or Latin.

     In other respects, however, FM must have presented a sharp
contrast to his youthful peers. That is, he was indifferent
to sports or physical exercise more strenuous than dancing
or walking, and he never learned to ride a horse properly
despite lessons in equestrianship. Moreover, by the time he
began his Diary, 1818, he had developed an extraordinary ap-
petite for reading, a habit he maintained throughout his
life. His reading, as we know from the earliest journal entries, included important works in Latin, Greek, French, and
Italian. He did not altogether shun theological books, so
numerous in that day, but the comments committed to his Diary

as well as his recorded reactions to sermons he heard in St. Thomas's Church suggest a less than lively concern with religion and probably a less than philosophical turn of mind.

Young FM received a formal education no better than that of his contemporaries in Portsmouth. At age four, he was sent in petticoats to a girls' school and then from ten to fifteen as a boarder to Bishops Waltham School, some miles distant. Thereafter, at his own volition, he continued at a day school kept by the Rev. H. Comyns at Portsea, and he also read Hebrew as a private pupil with a Mr. Sailman, "a Jew." His regular schooling, he noted, was broken off at Christmas, 1818 (D, 19 Oct. 1851).

Yet by this time he had become an amateur scholar, strongly drawn to languages and possessed of no small gifts in that field. Very likely, his cultivation of such studies and also the historical orientation of his reading were the result of his having whole-heartedly embraced the antiquarianism, the veneration of the past and especially of the Middle Ages, that was greatly in vogue at this time even in the provinces as a carry-over from the eighteenth century. Typically, the gentleman antiquary collected coins and seals, studied heraldry and genealogy, beginning with his own, rubbed brasses, copied inscriptions on tombs, sketched architectural details of old buildings, looked into the origins of folk customs, such as the chimney-sweeps' procession on 1 May, searched out local history, and sometimes even opened tumuli. The eighteen-year-old FM was already an active participant in such pursuits. But even the less inspired members of the military were touched by the antiquarian rage. Captain Madden, for example, had a collection of ancient coins, mainly Roman, which he gave to his youngest son in 1819, along with a handsome mahogany case, and FM for several years increased the collection as his slender means permitted.

Certain of these enthusiasms FM shared with his slightly older friend and confidant, Lake Allen. The two young men exchanged stilted Latin letters and planned various projects together, the most fruitful being a work of fiction based on records of a sixteenth-century Portsea churchwarden. FM, always more industrious and energetic than the sickly Allen, wrote the short story in December 1821, entitling it "Alice and Richard, a Local Tale," although he protested from the first that imaginative writing did not come naturally to him. Thus, he seems not to have been surprised or unduly downcast when the story was rejected by Colbourne's *New Monthly Magazine*.

Very soon after this experience, FM and Lake Allen learned that a Portsea printer, D.B. Price, was launching a periodi-

cal, *The Portsmouth, Portsea, and Gosport Literary and Scientific Register*, sixpence per issue, designed to attract
contributions on a wide range of subjects without compensation to the authors. The two young men were not impressed
by Price's qualifications as an editor and were aware that
his efforts to enroll influential subscribers had been largely unsuccessful. Nevertheless, in the first issue, dated 20
July 1822, is to be found FM's maiden publication, a three-
page letter addressed to "The Editor" and entitled "Antiquities." In the list of abbreviations above, an attempt is
made to explain the signature "Z," used at the end both of
this contribution and of another appearing the following
year. The letter "Antiquities," written in self-consciously
formal language, congratulates the editor for thus opening
to the inhabitants of the Portsmouth district the prospect
"of maintaining a place among the literary circles of the
age." The young author rejects the counsel of pedants who
cry "Procul, o profani!" as they refuse to share their
learning with others. He goes on to extol the study of antiquities and points out the few features of antiquarian interest in the area. To his Diary he confided his opinion
that his letter was the only contribution in the whole issue
worth reading (D, 20 June 1822).

Although Allen had earlier sought to dissuade FM from offering a single line to Price, he later approved of his send-
ing in the story rejected by the London magazine, and thus
"Alice and Richard" held pride of place in issue No. 2 of the
Register, 18 July 1822. Despite its sentimentality, this
tale of the young love of Alice Tottye and Richard Jervys,
their idyllic marriage, and then Alice's sudden death from
plague and the nearly simultaneous demise of Richard, struck
down by grief, is told better and more economically than
might be expected in that period. As indicated in the bibliography, "Alice and Richard" was reprinted by Price in
1840.

A different Madden is revealed in his two remaining publications in the *Register*, for "On the Origin and Progress of
Fairs" and the two-part "Warblington Castle and Church" are
research essays, clearly argued, less pretentiously written.
The soundness of FM's expository style at so early a date
surely owes much to the discipline of his almost daily journal entries. As we learn from the Diary, he had been think-
ing about the origin of fairs for some time before writing
his essay, whereas the Warblington topic appears to have been
suggested to him by Price.

Toward the close of his long "imprisonment" at home, to use
his own expression, FM's concern with local history and ar-

chaeology, coins, and the like came to be supplemented by a
rather suddenly awakened interest in medieval manuscripts.
He owed his introduction to manuscripts, and, incidentally,
the start of what was to be his career, to Lake Allen. This
young man, after a period in the office of the Portsmouth
clerk and coroner, was articled to a London solicitor, but
recurring bouts of illness made persevering in that calling
impossible. Thereupon, through family connections, he was
offered and accepted a post as manuscript copyist by Henry
Petrie, Keeper of Records at the Tower of London and director
of a great historical program sponsored by Parliament. "Oh
God! When will my turn arrive?" FM cried upon learning of
Allen's new employment (D, 13 June 1823). Allen's work, much
of it carried on in the British Museum, was often interrupted
by the wretched state of his health, and he was often obliged
to return to Portsmouth for recuperation. During such inter-
vals, FM was given the opportunity of examining his friend's
transcriptions and facsimiles of manuscripts, and he recorded
his pleasure in studying a few passages from the statutes of
Henry IV.

Such experiences intensified his dissatisfaction over
finding himself at age twenty-two still in his father's household, deprived of any preparation for a calling acceptable to
him. Captain Madden, aloof but probably not entirely the unfeeling man depicted in the Diary of this period, was puzzled
by this youth who found that Cicero inspired him to a life of
literary pursuits, who was set against following two of his
brothers into the armed services, and who was scornful of
settling for a civil servant's desk job, as his brother Henry
had done. Above all else, FM longed for a university education, probably with thoughts about taking orders and leading
the genteel life of his maternal grandfather, the Rochester
canon. Entering a university was an ambition that Captain
Madden refused to listen to, principally because the family
resources would scarcely permit the luxury of Oxford or Cambridge for his youngest son, and FM was obliged to mark time,
seething with unhappiness. Only in his Diary could he rail
against what he considered his father's stinginess and want
of sympathy.

His sudden deliverance from the parental trap may be dated
in December 1823 when, largely as a result of his mother's
initiative, he set out for London and the vicinity of Bath
to pay extended visits to his uncle, Sir George, his brothers
Henry and Lewis, and his mother's Powell relatives. At twenty-two years of age, FM reacted to his journey on the "Regu-
lator" coach and his first glimpse of London and his arrival
at the White Horse Cellar, Piccadilly, where Henry awaited

him, with the excitement of an adolescent, but thereafter the
Diary entries take on a note of maturity. Once settled in
Sir George's house in Cleveland Row, he spent relatively little time on the sights and amusements of the metropolis, although he was moved to comment on the revealing costumes of
ladies he saw at Drury Lane Theatre: "They might just as well
have taken off their clothes" (D, 12 Dec. 1823). With the
rather grudging cooperation of Lake Allen, he very soon
gained admission to the British Museum as a reader, and he
seems to have passed nearly every possible moment there during the remainder of his stay in London. In true Madden
fashion, he first studied the catalogue of Museum holdings,
then, after surveying the coin department and looking into
some genealogical books, he turned to manuscripts, beginning
with MS. Cotton Vespasian D. VII., the Middle English Psalter
from which he had seen a passage copied down by Allen. He
noted how inadequate were the available glossaries of early
English, a deficiency he even then felt a strong interest in
remedying. He likewise called for MS. Cotton Caligula A.
II., containing metrical romances, such as *Sir Launfal*.
While poring over these and other volumes, he noted how seldom Allen came into the Museum to perform his work, and he
was inclined to censure him ungenerously for a want of stami-
na.   It was at this moment that Henry, in one of his rare
bursts of family concern, proposed that he apply to Petrie
for a post similar to Lake Allen's, a suggestion that led to
a momentous interview and a demonstration of FM's competence
in reading a twelfth-century manuscript to Petrie's satis-
faction. This act brought about a cooling of an old friendship, and on poor Allen's part the resentment persisted during the brief remainder of his life.
     Fortune indeed favored FM in the succeeding weeks, for
while staying at Lewis's house in Batheaston, he met and was
cordially received by Lewis's near neighbor, the Rev. J.J.
Conybeare, one of the best Anglo-Saxonists in England and
lately Professor of Poetry at Oxford. Observing in his young
acquaintance the intentness of a born scholar, Conybeare,
"whose library would not have disgraced a nobleman" (D, 17
Jan. 1824), lent him books on Old English, such as William
Elstob's work on the Saxon Chronicle, and even some of his
personal collection of manuscripts. The two exchanged letters during the few months Conybeare had yet to live, and FM
was glad that he had written to express his gratitude to his
benefactor before his death in June 1824. As will appear,
Conybeare's encouragement, next to Petrie's, was of primary
importance in the shaping of FM's future. For example, it
was he who revived FM's early and then forlorn hope of en-

tering a university. A particularly crucial event fell on
FM's twenty-third birthday--that is, 16 February 1824--for
on that day he was notified that Petrie was ready to engage
him as an assistant. In April, he entered upon his new duties, first soliciting a gift of thirty pounds from his father to enable him to furnish a room in London. His initial
task was the transcription of a chronicle in MS. Cotton Caligula E. II.

FM continued as copyist for Petrie for more than four
years, including some months after he was made an officer of
the British Museum. He complained about the illiberal piece-
work remuneration, five pence per folio of seventy-two words,
yet he must have realized the immense value of the experience
he was accumulating. For his years of exacting work for
Petrie not only in the British Museum but in the other great
libraries and the muniment rooms of England gave him an ex-
pertise in palaeography scarcely matched by any scholar of
the century. Petrie himself was genuinely impressed by his
assistant and sought to forward his career. He was the first
to urge FM to publish *Havelok*, the manuscript of which he
had come across in the Bodleian Library, and also Layamon's
Brut, and it was from Petrie's hands that FM received his
certificate of membership in the Society of Antiquaries of
London. Moreover, it was through Petrie that he came to the
notice of Philip Bliss and J.B. Bandinell, both librarians
at Oxford, as well as Sir Francis Palgrave, the elderly Francis Douce, and other scholars. Dr. Bliss, who remained a
friend for many years, exerted himself a great deal on FM's
behalf, arranging for him to matriculate at Magdalen Hall,
Oxford, in July 1825 and to keep terms there on an irregular
basis. FM's need for earning his own way seriously inter-
fered with his progress in the university, and when he finally removed his name from the matriculation book in January
1831, he had not attained his B.A. degree. On the other
hand, by diligent study of logic, Herodotus, and other Greek
authors, he passed creditably his responsions or "little go"
in 1827.

FM's labors for Petrie in London and elsewhere during his
flirtation with a degree brought his talents to the notice
of several men of influence by whom he was encouraged to apply for an assistant librarianship in the Department of
Printed Books at the Museum. When in June 1826 this appointment fell to Henry Cary, already known for his translation of
Dante, he was much chagrined, but he was offered and accepted
part-time Museum employment as a cataloguer. Also, at the
beginning of 1826, he was ready to take up a congenial assignment, negotiations for which had begun the preceding No-

vember--the correction and completion of William Roscoe's
catalogue of the manuscripts at Holkham Hall, Norfolk, the
seat of Thomas Coke, who became Earl of Leicester in 1837.
Roscoe, talented and versatile but no bibliographer, was
aware of deficiencies in his attempt to survey the rich collection at Holkham, and, with the help of such scholars as
Sharon Turner and Sir Francis Palgrave, approached FM as one
with some experience with manuscripts, as explained in Mrs.
J.E. Graham's interesting essay on the subject.

FM was flattered by his courteous reception at Holkham
Hall, for he was treated as only slightly less than a guest
during his first visit, 1 to 26 March 1826, and he was happy
to return to finish the task the following spring, 12 March
to 10 April 1827. He found glaring inadequacies in Roscoe's
work and, with the occasional aid of Archdeacon George Glover,
rewrote the catalogue on a far more elaborate and professional scale. His finished product, in fact, proved to differ
so much from Roscoe's notion of a catalogue that publication
plans were canceled. FM received payments amounting to 350
pounds from Coke for his work, but he was angered that his
catalogue would not see print. Instead, his handwritten work
was bound in eight volumes and deposited at Holkham. Nearly
a century later, however, the then Lord Leicester permitted
Seymour de Ricci to abstract from the Roscoe-Madden catalogue
*A Handlist of the Manuscripts in the Library of the Earl of
Leicester at Holkham Hall*, published in 1932.

Few writers who have had occasion to refer to FM's sojourn
at Holkham Hall have failed to mention his amorous moments
with the young ("not yet 20") and famously beautiful Jane
Digby, Lady Ellenborough, Coke's granddaughter and wife of the
Lord Privy Seal. FM certainly more than hints at intimacies
with her: "... at midnight I escorted her to her room.--
Fool that I was!--I will not add what passed. Gracious God!
Was there ever such fortune!" (D, 24 Mar. 1827). It is interesting that another obsessive chronicler of his own life,
Thomas Creevey, M.P., was a guest at Holkham at the same
time. The gossipy Creevey took note of the presence both of
Lady Ellenborough, "the pretty Aurora, light of Day," and
also of FM, whom he refers to as "a young British Museum artist," but he seems not to have observed the two of them together. Several writers have traced the lurid adventures of
the lady following her divorce from Lord Ellenborough.

FM's real chance for stable employment did not come until
late in 1827 when the death of Joseph Planta, Principal Librarian, led to a series of changes. That is, Henry Ellis
succeeded to Planta's position, thus making way for Josiah
Forshall to become Keeper of Manuscripts. FM was thereupon

designated Assistant Keeper to Forshall, in part, at least,
because of his canvassing of Museum trustees, especially Lord
Spencer. Upon learning in February 1828 that his appointment
had at last been made official by the signatures of the Archbishop of Canterbury, the Lord Chancellor, and the Speaker of
the House of Commons, he exulted in his Diary: "Ita trium-
phales circa me tempora laure. Vicimus!" (D, 2 Feb. 1828).

The new subkeeper began his duties at once. Besides required attendance in the general reading room (a separate
room for readers of manuscripts was not provided until 1885),
he catalogued new accessions, attended sales of manuscripts
as a buyer, assisted in drawing up reports, and functioned in
such other capacities as listening to Sir Thomas Phillipps's
exorbitant terms for ceding his enormous collections to the
Museum and testifying as a handwriting expert in legal proceedings. He still carried out an occasional transcribing
task for Petrie, and he divided his vacation time between
reading Aeschylus at Oxford and courting Mary Hayton at
Brighton. Incredibly, in the same period he found time and
energy to devote to several scholarly projects.

His publications at that time included not only the four
contributions to Price's *Register* already mentioned, but also
certain variorum notes incorporated in an edition of Sueto-
nius published in 1826, an assignment he had secured upon
applying to the publisher, A.J. Valpy, for remunerative work.
He received forty-five pounds compensation, but his name did
not appear on the title page of the book. Again, in 1826, he
wrote out an analysis of the Latin plays of Hrotswitha at the
request of scholar named Whyte, or Bruce-Whyte. Pleased with
the results, Bruce-Whyte sent him an unexpected ten-pound
note, twenty shillings of which FM put to good use by buying
some caricatures for "M," that is, Mary Hayton. Bruce-Whyte's
Histoire des langues romanes, including FM's synopsis of
Hrotswitha's *Gallicanus*, was not published until 1841, however.

His first journal article, other than those appearing in
the *Register*, was published in the *Gentleman's Magazine* for
June 1825, a defense of Joseph Ritson against the attack made
on him by Richard Price in the latter's 1824 edition of Warton's *History of English Poetry*. This essay, signed "Rit-
sonianus," may be seen as an early enunciation of FM's devotion to meticulous accuracy in dealing with early manuscripts.

It is fair to say, however, that the publication in 1828
of *The Ancient English Romance of Havelok the Dane* marks the
true beginning of FM's scholarly career. Ever since coming
upon the long-mislaid manuscript of that romance (Bodleian
MS. Laud Misc. 108) in August 1825 (D, 12 Aug. 1825), and

especially after he was mentioned as the discoverer of the
manuscript in Conybeare's *Illustrations of Anglo-Saxon Poetry*
(D, 29 July 1826), he had contemplated an edition, and to
have it issued under the auspices of the Roxburghe Club was
for him a triumph. Perhaps the most significant factor in
this achievement was that FM, because of his thorough ground-
ing in Warton's *History of English Poetry* and in the works
of all the other early literary historians and editors, was
able to recognize instantly that he had indeed made a discovery when seeing the *Havelok* text. Although excellent from a
palaeographical point of view, FM's edition drew adverse critical reactions, some of them justifiable, from S.W. Singer
and John M. Kemble, as indicated in the commentary under this
title in the bibliography. As the result of Kemble's observations in particular, he was prompted to improve his knowledge of English philology.

Before completing three years as Assistant Keeper of Manuscripts, FM had established the intense pace of scholarly
activity that would be maintained for decades. Prior to the
appearance of his edition of the *Privy Purse Expenses of the
Princess Mary* in 1831, as may be seen in the bibliography,
he contributed nine articles to the *Gentleman's Magazine* and
seven to *Archaeologia*, the latter being papers presented before the Royal Society of Literature. A few of these studies
are on seals and other antiquarian *realia* but the greater
part describe and interpret documents bearing on medieval
history.

For a man barely out of his twenties who only six years
earlier languished in deep despair over his lack of any suit-
able occupation, such accomplishments were most gratifying.
Yet the third decade of FM's life closed with a shattering
tragedy, the death of his young wife and their child. The
moment his appointment as Assistant Keeper was assured, FM
set his marriage plans afoot in the face of less than warm
acquiescence on the part of Mary Hayton's mother, the unpleasant Mrs. Doolan. But the marriage was finally celebrated by the Rev. Mr. Bourn in St. George's Church, Bloomsbury,
on 18 March 1829. After a wedding trip by coach to Oxford
and elsewhere, the Maddens settled down in their Museum apartment, and there followed a round of visiting and modest en-
tertainments. In October, the new husband jotted down in
his Diary a Latin note referring to Mary's pregnancy (D, 13
Oct. 1829). Few months of wedded happiness were left: Mary
was confined the last week of the following February but
after parturition died of puerperal fever. The infant, although at first seemingly healthy, weakened rapidly and after
a hurried baptism as Frederick Hayton by the Rev. Josiah

Forshall died and was interred with his mother. Still to be seen in the nave of St. George's Church is the memorial tablet surmounted by a grieving angel which FM caused to be erected to his wife and son. As we learn from the Diary, the monument originally bore a long and effusive inscription, but in 1862 this was expunged and replaced by the present subdued and dignified tribute, including a short passage in Greek (D, 4 May 1830; 2 Dec. 1862).

The fulsome rhetoric of grief in vogue during the earlier decades of the century is reflected not only in the original inscription on Mary Hayton's monument but in many entries in the Diary as well. Especially on the anniversaries of her birth and death, FM was prone to outbursts such as "Oh God! There are no curses deep enough to relieve my heart from the anguish caused by the memory of that sweet girl's fate!" (D, 26 Feb. 1841). One practical consequence of his loss was his abandonment of his struggle to attain an Oxford degree, a venture begun, he once stated, by Mary's wish that he take Holy Orders. He was frank enough to admit, however, that he could no longer submit to reading Sophocles and Thucydides merely in order to add "an empty A.M. to my name."

Freed from this distraction, he devoted himself to his Museum duties and, in the remaining time, to his scholarly labors. In August 1831, the *Privy Purse Expenses of the Princess Mary* was published, a volume of some three hundred pages on which he had been working seriously for several years. But, as he was completing this task, sponsors for three other large editing projects materialized. First, John Campbell, Earl of Cawdor, arranged late in 1830 for the publication by the Roxburghe Club of an edition of *William and the Werwolf* (D, 14 Nov. 1830), a volume which made its appearance in 1832. Second, at about this time, the delegates of the Oxford University Press entered into an agreement with Josiah Forshall and FM to publish an edition of the complete Wycliffite Bible (D, 26 Mar. 1831), an enormous undertaking which did not reach fruition until 1850. And third, the Society of Antiquaries authorized FM to proceed with a two-text edition of Layamon's *Brut* (D, 16 Sept. 1831), which was finally completed in 1847. During the years that followed, he was obliged to turn somewhat frantically from one of these commitments to another, yet he was not deterred from adding still another responsibility in 1836, the preparation of *Syr Gawayne, a Collection of Ancient Romance-Poems* (D, 25 Aug. 1836), published by the Bannatyne Club in 1839. The evolution of this famous work, which began in 1829 with FM's examination of the unique manuscript of *Sir Gawain and the Green Knight* and included two interviews with Sir Walter Scott, is traced in the bibliography.

The bibliography also shows that FM throughout this period continued to contribute papers to the *Gentleman's Magazine* and *Archaeologia*, one of the most interesting being a two-part history of chess, which includes an account of the ancient walrus-ivory chessmen recently discovered on the island of Lewis.

One more endeavor of these years--the planning and launching, along with Sir Thomas Phillipps, Sir Francis Palgrave, Charles Young, and the Rev. Joseph Hunter, of a periodical, *Collectanea Topographica et Genealogica*--preempted no insignificant portion of FM's attention beginning early in 1831. As described in the prospectus written by FM, the new journal would be devoted to the publication of hitherto inedited documents of historical interest, especially those pertaining to old parishes and manors, ancient population figures, scutage rolls, monastic cartularies, the descent of important families, and the like (D, 30 June 1831, etc.). The founders would serve as editors, and the *Collectanea* would be published in quarterly issues at a price of five shillings. The two hundred subscribers, a number which altered very little during the life of the journal, were nearly all members of the Society of Antiquaries, and some were authors of regional and local histories. Despite the limited subscription list, the *Collectanea* was published regularly from 1834 through 1841, although FM came to play a less active role in its production after the first two years.

In some ways, especially in its emphasis on local history and genealogy, the *Collectanea* harks back to the days of the gentleman antiquary. The most consistent and prolific contributor, "C.G.Y.," whom we can identify as Sir Charles Young, York Herald at the College of Arms, concentrated on additions to Dugdale's *The Baronage of England* (1675-76). Indeed, *the Gentleman's Magazine* declared that his many emendations to Dugdale's famous work would alone justify the existence of the new journal. To draw up an accurate list of FM's contributions is not easy, because of variations in the initials used to acknowledge authorship. The obituary read before the Royal Society of Literature credits him with ten *Collectanea* articles without noting that, of these, four appeared in successive installments. But, on the basis of the Diary and other evidence, we are safe in assigning several additional papers to him.

The intensity of FM's mourning for his wife and son may suggest that he immersed himself in scholarship as a form of therapy. At the same time, he seems to have discharged his duties in the Museum creditably enough. In particular, he was active in obtaining new accessions for his department by attendance at manuscript sales, and he also made an appearance before the House of Lords to give testimony about certain charters. All historians of the British Museum emphasize that FM's acerb disposition, his insistence on his prerogatives, and his arrogance toward those he considered his social or intellectual inferiors impaired his effectiveness as an administrative officer. We may note, however, that these same historians do not always give sufficient recognition to the great service he rendered the Museum and the nation in his career-long dedication to identifying and restoring to readable condition the many damaged and neglected manuscripts of the priceless Cotton Collection. The Cotton Manuscripts, in a sense the nucleus of the Museum Library, had suffered grievously in a fire at Ashburnham House in October 1731 as the result of which many manuscripts were listed as lost in the catalogues of Casley (1734) and Planta (1802). Not only in the course of his regular duties but also for the sake of forwarding such of his own projects as the editing of Layamon's *Brut*, FM faced squarely, as his predecessors had failed to do, the problem presented by the congealed lumps of vellum fragments still preserved from the fire, and very early he began the arduous work of rehabilitation.

Gradually at first, then with increasing frequency and zest, FM began going out into society, thus signaling the end of his mourning. He attended not only meetings of the Royal Society and the Antiquaries but also balls and dinners and *conversazioni*, such as those held by the Duke of Sussex at Kensington Palace. He also confesses, sometimes in detail, to a series of encounters with emancipated, or at least available, women, ranging from street-girls to more sophisticated demi-mondaines. Certain of these women proved troublesome to him over the years, particularly one Kerry Bradshaw. Another, primarily the mistress of a much wealthier man, declared that he was the father of her child born in 1835. Much later he took the pains to meet the child in question, then sixteen, concluding that he could not have fathered an offspring who resembled him so little. By purchasing a horse and cab and engaging a groom, or "tiger," he tried earnestly to present the image of a man-about-town. This venture proved unfortunate, for his touch with horses had not changed for the better. The first animal he bought was found almost at once to have a "nerved" foreleg and had to be sold at a considerable loss. On one occasion when he drove out alone (he had never before held a whip, he admits), he splintered a shaft on a gate post in front of his brother Henry's house, and not long afterwards a serious accident was

narrowly averted when a woman and child strayed into the path
of his vehicle. Finally in 1837 he sent his horse away to
be sold for thirty-five pounds and also disposed of his cab.
His close association with horses ended at this point except
for occasional riding lessons with his sons years later.

With three substantial books and many well-received papers
to his credit, FM at age thirty-one was justly regarded as a
scholar of some eminence and of even greater promise. He
was elected not only to the Society of Antiquaries, the Royal
Society of Literature, and the Archaeological Society, but
also to the newly founded Athenaeum Club, the Royal Irish
Academy, the Royal Society of Copenhagen, and the like, in
the first two of which he was also a fellow. Moreover, the
many new scholarly organizations that blossomed during his
lifetime sought to strengthen their prestige by use of his
name. Among these were the Camden Society, which he thought
might better have been named after Sir Robert Cotton, the
Aelfric Society, the Philological Society of London, and,
toward the close of his days, the Early English Text Society.
Among his friends and admirers he could count the keepers of
records in the Tower of London and the College of Arms and
even in the 1830's such men as Sir Thomas Phillipps, Bart.,
and peers like Lord Spencer, Lord Cawdor, and the Bishop of
Llandaff.

That he should have considered himself worthy of a knighthood is not surprising given that among his friends in analogous posts, including predecessors and contemporaries in
the Museum, not a few had been included in the honors lists
on the basis of comparatively meager achievements. Moreover,
in his cynical moments, he looked upon a knighthood as the
surest avenue to a financially and socially advantageous second marriage. His campaign of soliciting support in this ambition from acquaintances seems shameless today, but in this
respect he was merely conforming to custom. His persistence
was rewarded, for in 1832 he was designated a Companion of
the Hanoverian Guelphic Order, and on 13 March 1833, attired
in a court costume he could ill afford, he drove to St.
James's Palace in a carriage borrowed from Lady Martin, a
relative, where King William IV rather casually dubbed him
Sir Frederic, Knight of the same order (D, 30 July 1832; 13
Mar. 1833). His social position thus enhanced, he continued
his somewhat awkward efforts to live up to the racy code of
a Regency gentleman, although the expense was greater than
he could bear. For example, he accepted membership in the
Star Club, a society of single gentlemen who donned a dis-
tinctive uniform when dining together, but he soon found his
fellow members boring, and resigned. His several liaisons

in this period often made him miserable, and he more than once acknowledged that he was "tired to death of raking."

In his quest for a rich and well, if not nobly, born wife, FM went so far in 1833 and 1834 as to pay court to a great heiress, Miss Duffield, to whom his wealthy Powell relatives had introduced him. The young lady was unmoved, however, and in the end rebuffed him pointedly, an experience her suitor tried to take in the "vogue la galère" spirit of the Regency beau. Not long afterwards, he met "pretty Miss Robinson" at a ball, and he was soon escorting her on walks in the public gardens and, after calling on her parents in Tottenham, to church and even, properly chaperoned, to the Lord Mayor's ball in the Guildhall. Emily Sarah Robinson's father was a magistrate and deputy lieutenant for the County of Middlesex who, generally called "doctor" in recognition of his Scottish Ll.D. degree, was a substantial citizen rather than the magnate FM had vaguely hoped for in a new father-in-law. Dr. William Robinson also wrote and published privately works on local history that FM found unimpressive. Love ripened between Emily and Frederic, encouraged by Mrs. Robinson, but marriage did not become possible until September 1837, by which time FM had been advanced in salary and dignity to the post of Keeper of Manuscripts. Before the wedding day, he was just able to disentangle himself from his liaisons, although Kerry Bradshaw thereafter sent him two unsigned letters, one alluding to his supposed illegitimate child. This letter he showed to Emily and, even more incredibly, he turned over to his bride, for her edification, his Diary for the years 1819 to 1829, but her reactions are not chronicled.

The publications of the period 1832 to 1840 are very numerous and include several of FM's most significant contributions. In addition to his splendid *Syr Gawayne* of 1839, already mentioned, he produced his edition of the little treatise *How the Goode Wif Thaught hir Doughter* (1837) and *The Old English Versions of the Gesta Romanorum* (1838), utilizing for the latter a manuscript he had first seen in Conybeare's library in 1824. Further, he provided the descriptions of manuscript pages reproduced in Henry Shaw's beautiful *Illuminated Ornaments Selected from Manuscripts and Early Printed Books* (1833), and he claimed a part, albeit unacknowledged, in a Camden Society publication, John Gage Rokewode's edition of the *Chronica Jocelin de Brakelonda* (1840). By no means negligible are the corrections and many additions which FM supplied to Taylor's 1840 edition of Warton's *History of English Poetry*. Thirty years later, W. Carew Hazlitt remarked that the chief improvement in Taylor's edition over that of Price, which had appeared in 1824, consisted of FM's notes to Volume I, dealing with Old and Middle English literature.

In the flood of articles of these years, a paper read before the Society of Antiquaries in 1837 and printed soon thereafter aroused particular attention and no little controversy, as indicated in the bibliography. For here FM argued strongly for the acceptance of the spelling "Shakspere" on the basis of certain documents. Another essay, "On the Progress of Anglo-Saxon Literature in England," 1834, is important because FM frankly admits to the justice of some of J.M. Kemble's strictures about the ignorance of Old English on the part of medievalists. All this while, it should be remembered, he was continuing the collation of the many copies of the Wycliffite Bible with relatively little help from the afflicted Forshall, and also the labor of editing and translating the two Layamon texts.

The new marriage, a success for the start, was all that FM could have hoped for, except that it did not bring him a fortune. As the highly personable Lady Madden, an impression reinforced by later photographs of her pasted into the Diary, Emily maintained a good relationship with the families of other Museum officers, such as the Hawkinses and Grays, who also lived in apartments on the premises, entertained graciously, and was at least as much interested as her husband in the panorama of London life, including Victoria's coronation. For this momentous event, FM arranged for Emily and several members of the Robinson family to view the procession from the windows of the Athenaeum Club. As a Gentleman of the Privy Chamber, a rather empty honor which he had been accorded in 1837, FM had a seat in Westminster Abbey. From that vantage point, which he assumed at 6:00 A.M. on 28 June 1837, he could observe every moment of the ceremony, and he secured one of the silver medals thrown among the peers and maids of honor, as he reported in a full and vivid Diary entry (D, 28 June 1837).

Lady Madden smoothly worked her husband into family gatherings, including the annual Christmas parties at Tottenham, and to all appearances remained cheerful and equable and perhaps even high spirited throughout her life, a refreshing contrast to FM. So far as may be seen from the record, she ran her household unobtrusively and organized the family vacation sojourns at such places as Leamington, Bath, Brighton, and the Isle of Wight with careful regard for her spouse's almost unremitting work schedule.

A breathing space before children began arriving allowed her during the summer of 1838 to accompany FM on a library tour of France and Belgium, the first continental trip for both. In Paris they were sought out by scholars such as Michel, Champollion, and Paulin Paris, they attended the op-

era, they viewed not only the libraries but the Louvre, the
Tuileries Gardens, and Sainte Chapelle, and were received by
Guizot, the Minister of Education. Eight years later, Emily,
accompanied by her sister Charlotte, joined her husband and
his assistant Holmes on a second trip. On this occasion, FM
visited the Bibliothèque du Roi, but his principal objective
was to examine manuscripts offered for sale by Count Libri.
The first child, born 9 April 1839, was christened Frederic
William. George Ernest Phillipps Madden, who owed one of
his names to his godfather, Sir Thomas Phillipps, was born
17 June 1841. Charles James appeared in 1843 and a fourth
boy, Henry, two years later, but both were dead of various
ailments by February 1846. No doubt, Emily's trip to France
later that year was a means of assuaging her grief. The only
girl, Emily Mary, was born in April 1848, and the last child,
James Arnold Wycliffe, in 1850, the year of the completion of
the Bible of John Wycliffe.

In the decade preceding 1850, a major event was the publication of *Laȝamons Brut*. After prodding from the Society
of Antiquaries, to which FM responded irascibly, for he went
so far as to tender his resignation as a fellow of that or-
ganization (D, 19 May 1845), he brought his monumental book
to a close. Because of the almost faultless editing of the
two texts, one of them a badly damaged manuscript which he
had helped to restore, and also the soundness of the translation and glossary, this three-volume work is properly considered one of the great scholarly achievements of the century. A similar status may be accorded, despite later cri-
ticism, to the Wycliffite Bible which appeared just three
years after. As indicated in Bibliography A, a critical edition of the Bible was set afoot by Baber, while Keeper of
Printed Books at the Museum, with the collaboration of Josiah
Forshall, but upon Baber's withdrawal in 1829, FM was asked
to assume his burden. Then, as the result of Forshall's
occasional bouts of mental illness, the greater share of the
exacting work of collating some 170 manuscripts in many libraries and private collections had to be borne by FM, and
the same was true of the writing of the preface and critical
apparatus. With good reason he rejoiced at the conclusion
of his twenty-one years of labor (D, 18 Oct. 1850). It may
be added that FM, having ordered his own copy of the finished
work to be bound in purple morocco, presented it to Prince
Albert as an expression of his gratitude for the Consort's
recommendation of young Fritz Madden for a scholarship at
Charterhouse (D, 4 Dec. 1850; 18 Jan. 1851).

The year 1850 saw the publication also of FM's translation,
with corrections, of Silvestre's *Fac-similes of Writings*

of all Nations and Periods, a contribution to palaeographical
study of some value in its day.

A conscientious and sometimes a fond father, FM came to
feel disappointed in his two older sons, for neither Frederic
William, called Fritz, nor George proved capable of living
up to his academic expectations in the excellent schools in
which they were optimistically enrolled (St. Paul's, Merchant
Tailor's, Charterhouse, and several less prestigious institu-
tions). George, always FM's favorite despite his wayward-
ness, was even less successful than Fritz, but he passed his
examinations for the Horse Guards, whereupon his father purchased for him a commission as ensign for 450 pounds, a large
outlay for the family. Arnold, as the youngest surviving son
came to be called, performed very well at Merchant Tailor's,
winning a scholarship at St. John's, Oxford. Once in university, however, his zeal flagged seriously, although he was
applying himself to the study of law with apparent diligence
at the time of his father's death. Emily Mary was a source
of comfort and gratification to her parents and not least
when, at the age of twenty-two, she married the gentlemanly
Col. Tedlie.

The Madden family, like any other, experienced cares and
sorrows. The death of children and parents, the financial
straits of near relatives, the mental illness of Emma Madden,
the only sister of whom FM was genuinely fond, and the senile
behavior of his oldest sister, Maria, are all meticulously
recorded. An unpleasant entanglement, which we know of only
because FM chose to speak about it in his Diary, was the
clandestine, intermittent affair he carried on with an un-
married sister-in-law, Charlotte, who died in 1867. The demise of his crotchety brother Henry in 1863 at the age of
seventy affected FM more than one would expect in view of the
coolness that had arisen several times between the two. But
as the recipient of a good share of Henry's unexpectedly substantial estate, FM must have felt in a sounder position to
contemplate retirement not long thereafter.

With the Wycliffite Bible off his hands, FM seemed content
to slacken his exertions to some extent. That, even so, he
was far from idle is suggested by the more than twenty papers
and short notes on a variety of subjects published during the
1850's. These range from items in the newly founded *Notes &
Queries* to longer contributions in the *Archaeological Journal*.
He also participated in the early stages of a most important
development, the full impact of which has been felt only in
recent decades, the photographing of manuscript material. In
November 1852, W.J. Thoms called at the Museum with a photograph of a medieval cartulary leaf that had been executed by

a Dr. Diamond, and he discussed with FM the great advantages
of this method of reproducing manuscripts over the method of
tracing. FM was at once enthusiastic and could foresee the
day when "accurate facsimiles of any number of pages of a
MS. ... may be taken without difficulty and at trifling expense" (D, 6 Nov. 1852). He also inserted in his Diary,
where it may still be seen, the reduced photograph given him
by Thoms. Then, in February 1856, Professor Selwyn secured
permission from the Museum Trustees to have photographs made
of certain leaves of the precious Codex Alexandrinus, a
fifth-century Greek Bible that had been acquired by the Royal
Library in 1627. The vellum leaves in question contain the
unique copy of two of the Epistles of Clement of Rome to the
Corinthians, highly regarded and generally regarded as canon-
ical by early Christians. The Clementine Epistles had already been edited more than once, but the realization that
the manuscript leaves were deteriorating rapidly lent some
urgency to the making of a photographic copy. Accordingly,
Roger Fenton, "photographic artist," set up his equipment on
the leads of the Museum building where, partly under FM's
supervision, the work was completed in April. Panizzi, very
recently elevated to the post of Principal Librarian, glanced
at the results, observing that manuscripts should still be
traced, an instance of obtuseness which did not fail to rouse
FM's ire. In October of that same year, FM prepared a brief
preface offering a word of explanation about the Clementine
Epistles and the work of photographing the manuscript. The
preface was then bound up with the photographs, listed as
edited by FM's assistant, William Cureton.

In 1858, FM was persuaded by the Master of Rolls to under-
take the editing of the minor chronicle of Matthew Paris, in
which he had long before taken an interest. He tried thereafter to resume his old schedule of working almost nightly
in his study from 8:00 to 11:30, but the labor of transcription and collation was less easily endured, and he confessed
to weariness from time to time. After suffering reminders
from the Master of Rolls, he brought the third and final volume to completion in late 1868, nearly three years after his
retirement.

Museum life after 1850 was if anything more strenuous and
exacerbating than ever. In carrying out his responsibilities, FM was assisted by such men as William Cureton, John
Holmes, Nicholas Hamilton, Edward Bond, and Edward Maunde
Thompson, but his duties were numerous and time-consuming.
These included the searching out and purchasing of manuscripts as funds were available, dealing with personnel problems, supervising the preparation of catalogues, writing re-

ports to the Principal Librarian and the Trustees, and even
overseeing drills with the Museum fire-fighting equipment,
the "engines," to use FM's term. One considerable service he
rendered his department was his thorough-going revision of
Samuel Ayscough's catalogue of the Sloane, Birch, and Additional manuscripts from 1 to 5017 (1782). Long before, he
had noted that the usefulness of this work was limited by
Ayscough's plan of classifying his entries according to the
varied contents of the manuscripts, with the result that only
with great difficulty could one discover what was included in
any individual manuscript. He had also found many errors in
this "villainous" work and for some time had wished to cor-
rect it but "wanted the heart to attempt it" (D, 3-9 Feb.
1857). At last, in February 1857, he took two copies of
Ayscough to his study where, with considerable help from
Emily, he cut out Ayscough's twenty thousand entries and re-
arranged them in strictly numerical order, at the same time
making corrections. This work required a firsthand knowledge
of the manuscripts themselves; consequently, it could not
have been left to clerical assistants or the binders. In a
spirit of resignation, FM noted that he could expect no
thanks from the Trustees for this labor even if he were to
inform them about it (D, 9 Feb. 1857).

His self-imposed task of restoring the Cotton Collection
continued into 1864, in which year he declared the project
at an end. In his farewell letter to the Trustees, he rests
his claim to recognition mainly on his salvaging, rendering
legible, and identifying the mutilated remnants of the fire
of 1731: "it is not too much for me to say that after a
lapse of more than twenty years, I may claim without egotism
the title of Restorer of the Cottonian Library" (D, 12 July
1866). Consisting originally of 958 volumes of manuscripts,
according to Thomas Smith's catalogue of 1696, the collection
was reduced by the fire to 861 volumes, many of those in a
damaged state, as indicated in Casley's register of 1734.
The remaining 97 Casley considered to be lost forever. During his long service in the Museum, 1776-1827, Planta was
able to improve upon fifty-one damaged volumes, but Forshall,
his successor, made little further progress. Soon after taking office as Keeper, FM began working both with bundles of
soaked and burnt vellum that had long been kept in cases in
his department and also with an accumulation of charred
scraps he discovered in a garret of the Museum. Under his
direction, workmen peeled the shriveled leaves from the lumps
of congealed vellum and afterwards flattened and "inlaid"
them--that is, pieced the fragments together on larger sheets
of paper. FM then collated the leaves and sought to identify
the "lost" works to which they belonged. The volumes

sometimes wholly reconstituted could now be sent to the
bindery. The hand labor was great, but the identification
was a particularly exacting operation calling for a depth of
learning possessed by few besides FM. He rejoiced when he
was able to reassemble literary or historical writings, such
as the chronicle of Higden in MS. Otho D. I. (MSS. Otho D. I.
and D. II. were both given up for lost ["desiderantur"] in
Planta's catalogue). He further restored a good part of MS.
Otho C. XIII., the later Layamon text, although Forshall before him had chanced on a few leaves. The magnitude of FM's
restoration is best reflected in his terse entries in the
margins of his office copy of Planta. In all, as he reported
in 1864, 927 of the Cottonian manuscripts were then available
to readers as contrasted with Planta's 861. At the same
time, FM corrected erroneous descriptions of long standing.
The best example, perhaps, is provided by MS. Cotton Nero A.
X. which, like his predecessors, Planta described as containing a single Old English poem on moral subjects. Such a
statement concealed, of course, the existence in the manuscript of four great Middle English poems, *Pearl*, *Sir Gawain
and the Green Knight*, *Cleanness*, and *Patience*. It should be
acknowledged, however, that Richard Price, in his 1824 edition of Warton's *History of English Poetry*, preceded FM in
pointing out the separate poems in this manuscript.

On one occasion, FM spoke of "his friend, Mr. Panizzi of
the British Museum," but this was in a footnote appearing in
his early work, the *Privy Purse Expenses of the Princess Mary*
(1831), in which he acknowledges Panizzi's corrections of
his rendering of an Italian passage. But basically he was
always hostilely disposed and his feelings were not seldom
fanned into flame. Especially embittering was his long and
ultimately unsuccessful struggle to retain the custody of the
manuscripts forming part of the library of Thomas Grenville,
which came to the Museum in 1847. The story of this conflict
has been related by Miller and others, with emphasis on FM's
pettiness and intransigence and with less acknowledgment of
Panizzi's very similar qualities and his vindictiveness than
may be entirely just. It suffices to say here that FM was
finally in 1851 obliged to surrender the prize Grenville
manuscript, the illustrations of Julius Clovio, yet we find
him still protesting the disposition of the matter as late
as 1860. Panizzi's rise to the Principal Librarianship in
1856 as Sir Henry Ellis's successor was the second great de-
feat. FM had put himself forward for that position and was
almost mortally offended by certain of his friends, notably
Sir Thomas Phillipps, who failed to support his application
with the enthusiasm he felt was his due. But in his fierce

opposition to Panizzi's elevation he was by no means alone,
for Panizzi had incurred the bad will of a number of his colleagues and not only because of his foreign birth. Nor did
FM's hatred spring solely from the fact that, by chance,
Panizzi's appointment to the Museum in 1828 antedated his
own by two days. Once Panizzi assumed his new office, FM
burned with even greater indignation. He is reported to have
been willing to communicate with his new chief only through
an assistant, and he churlishly absented himself from the celebration marking the opening in 1865 of the great domed
reading room, designed by Panizzi. The appearance over the
door to the reading room of a bust of the Principal Librarian, in place of a bust of Minerva or of Queen Victoria proposed by the architect, Sir Robert Smirke, was especially
galling.

    FM had already decided that the great circular room, al-
though splendid in appearance, was "perfectly unsuited ...
to its purpose." One must remember, however, that users of
manuscripts still sat in the same room as readers of printed
material, a situation that prevailed until long after FM's
death. Because of the inevitably looser surveillance of
readers in the vast new addition, FM was properly concerned
over the safety of his manuscripts, and at last he succeeded
in setting up special regulations as a safeguard.

    In consequence of his position, FM was approached sooner
or later by nearly every vendor of manuscripts in Europe,
legitimate and otherwise. As revealed in his correspondence
and the Diary, he was alert to the possibility of theft and
forgery and thus he seems at no time to have been seriously
victimized, as was Sir Thomas Phillipps on occasion. Two of
his more interesting early experiences have been discussed
by Winstanley and thus may be summarily treated here. The
first, which took place early in 1845, involved James Orchard
Halliwell, later Halliwell-Phillipps, who was suspected of
having purloined from Trinity College, Cambridge, a manuscript later purchased by the Museum. After conferring with
the Master of Trinity College and Sir Henry Ellis, FM laid
the matter before the Trustees, who, in company with Trinity
College, brought suit against Halliwell. To FM's disgust,
the case was dropped for want of sufficient evidence, and the
suspect went on to become a prolific and widely respected
scholar. It is interesting to note that Halliwell became
Halliwell-Phillipps after marriage in 1842 to Sir Thomas
Phillipps's eldest daughter, the same young lady who had been
urged on FM some years before (D, 13 Oct. 1831).

    The second experience was with Count Libri, whose Paris
lodgings, crammed with evil-smelling vellum manuscripts, FM

had visited along with Holmes in May 1846. Libri was a dealer of questionable reputation, and FM was outraged, when, in
1859, the Count refused to take back a Galileo manuscript he
had misrepresented. In 1853 and 1854, FM encountered yet
another thief, George Hillier, as Edwards and Hockey have
shown. In October 1854, FM noted that he finally had proof
that Hillier was a villain who had stolen manuscripts from
Lord Mostyn and Lord Ellesmere (D, 10 Oct. 1854).

A Greek, Constantine Simonides, a far bolder if less dis-
creet scoundrel, was first introduced at the Museum by an in-
terpreter from the Foreign Office in February 1853. Among
the manuscripts he offered for sale, scrolls of classical authors and of imperial rescripts, FM observed at once that
some were highly suspect, and he later recalled having read
about the exposure of similar frauds in Athens the year before. In fact, as Munby points out in his "Phillipps Studies," No. 3, a commission in Athens found that Simonides'
scroll of the *Iliad* was taken from Wolff's recent edition of
that work, complete with errata. Phillipps bought from Simonides the Hesiod scroll which FM had seen at once to be a
forgery, whereas FM himself purchased only some genuine Bib-
lical manuscripts. In 1856, the newspapers reported that
Simonides had been arrested in Leipzig on the charge of sell-
ing a forgery to the Berlin Academy, whereupon the *Athenaeum*
in London published an article suggesting that the British
Museum had been similarly duped by the same man. FM's indig-
nant rebuttal of this "shabby and base lie" appeared in a
subsequent number of the *Athenaeum* and the tempest subsided.
Refusing to admit to wrongdoing, Simonides was said to have
claimed that the great mid-fourth-century Codex Sinaiticus,
brought from Mt. Sinai by Tischendorf, sold to the Russian
government, and finally acquired by the British Museum in
1933, was actually his own handiwork. At last, in 1863, he
had the still greater audacity to maintain his innocence of all
charges of dishonest dealing before the Royal Society of Literature. The meeting was raucous and apparently ended in his
total humiliation (D, 7, 9, 19 Jan. 1863).

During the period when Simonides still had such supporters
as Sir Thomas Phillipps, FM discovered, as did others, that
John Payne Collier, eminent as a Shakespeare scholar, was
also a forger. Collier had sought to justify certain of his
emendations, which in themselves were often very good, by
writing the changes in his copy of the second Shakespeare
folio in what he hoped would be taken as a seventeenth-cen-
tury hand. FM was far from elated on confronting proof of
these forgeries and declined to publish his findings over his
own name, "after so many years of friendship." Instead, he

let others set forth the evidence, in particular his assistant, N.E.S.A. Hamilton.

In 1857 Emily and the boys accompanied FM on his last
trip to the Continent, this time to Cologne, Aix-la-Chapelle,
and Boulogne, and it is interesting to note that he allowed
himself much more time for sight-seeing than on his previous
journeys. In the next decade there were few such happy periods. In 1865, young George, invalided home from Canada, evidently as the result of syphilis, died miserably only a few
days after brightly wishing his father a happy birthday. FM
was broken by this loss, and his grief tormented him the remainder of his days. In July, a fire in Tuckett's bindery
damaged a number of manuscripts awaiting binding, including
several of the Cotton vellums on which FM and his staff had
expended much effort.

In the same month as the fire came reports of Panizzi's
imminent retirement, together with newspaper speculation
about his possible successor. FM was occasionally mentioned
in this connection, a fact which encouraged him to write letters of application both then and at the close of the year.
But, early in 1866, he advised Sir Thomas Phillipps of his
intention to follow Panizzi in retirement should a junior officer be selected over his head as the new Principal Librarian. Thus, when notified at mid-year of the appointment of
John Winter Jones, Keeper of Printed Books, he quietly noted
in his Diary that, with Emily's concurrence, he would resign.
The letter of resignation, containing, as already indicated,
an allusion to his restoration of the Cotton Collection, was
submitted 12 July and within two weeks was accepted by the
Trustees, simultaneously with Panizzi's resignation. FM was
angered upon learning that no special bonus would be added
to his regular retirement pension of six hundred pounds per
year whereas Panizzi was treated far more liberally, as
Borrie has noted. His last day of service was 29 September,
and within two months he and Emily had moved their family
and household possessions, including three thousand books,
out of their Museum apartment into a relatively new house at
25 St. Stephens Street, Bayswater, which they leased for 120
pounds per annum.

Even though FM protested occasionally that retirement did
not bring contentment or consolation, a lightening of spirits
clearly attended the move to the rather spacious house in a
then new and respectable neighborhood. Freed from the routine obligations to which he had been tied for forty years,
FM soon resumed work on his Matthew Paris chronicle and found
time to index the earlier volumes of his Diary and sort over
correspondence and other papers. A few new friendships

proved gratifying. One was with the Rev. Walter W. Skeat
who, at the outset of his scholarly activities, opened what
came to be a fairly busy correspondence when he wrote to beg
FM's assistance in preparing a new edition of *William and the
Werwolf* for the Early English Text Society. Later, Skeat re-
edited *Havelok* for the same series, paying heart-warming tribute in his introduction to FM's pioneer work. FM responded
eagerly to such praise, couched as it was in a "gentlemanly
tone." As he noted in 1868, it was strange that, given the
many communications between them, the two men never met.

Relations with another medievalist, Frederick J. Furnivall,
who for productiveness and prominence came to rival Halliwell-
Phillipps and Skeat, were very different. In 1861, Furnivall
called on FM in the Museum to consult him about his work on
Manuel des Péchés and also the *Sankgreall*. FM was unimpressed,
and he observed privately that he questioned Furnivall's
capacity as an editor. His misgivings acquired a touch of
annoyance the following year when Furnivall requested that
he provide dates of composition for a long list of Middle
English romances and several other works for the sake of "our
dictionary"--that is, *The New English Dictionary* planned by
the Philological Society of London. Nevertheless, FM recom-
mended Furnivall's appointment as Professor of English Literature at King's College, observing in his Diary that he did
not object to speaking well of the man. But soon thereafter,
upon learning that Furnivall had endorsed William Stubbs instead of himself as the new Principal Librarian, his distrust
became acute. He not only gave vent to his injured feelings
in a letter but returned unopened the gift copy of Furnivall's
Queste du Seynt Graal, published by the Roxburghe Club. Evidently a rather irrepressible man, Furnivall remained unruf-
fled and thereafter wrote FM from time to time as though nothing were amiss.

A much more pleasant if distant association resulted from
correspondence and a conversation with W. Carew Hazlitt,
grandson of the essayist, in 1868 and 1869. Having undertak-
en yet another edition of the venerable *History of English
Poetry* by Warton, Hazlitt asked simply for any notes FM may
not have utilized in the Taylor edition of 1840, and, favor-
ably impressed, FM complied. When in May 1871 Hazlitt sent
him the four volumes of the new Warton with a note apologiz-
ing for his inability to give the work away, he philosophi-
cally sent him a check at once. On a less frequent basis,
FM exchanged letters with Richard Morris, the editor of the
first publication of the Early English Text Society, with
Oswald Cockayne, and with Paulin Paris, who sent him a copy
of his *Romans de Table Ronde*. He further subjected weighty

books like Edward Freeman's *History of the Norman Conquest* to
the same critical reading that is reflected in the précis and
evaluations of his reading to be found in the early years of
his Diary. The post-mortem appearance in print of the journal of an acquaintance, Henry Crabb Robinson, prompted him to
draw comparisons with his own Diary. In general, he regarded
the record of Robinson's life as dull and trivial, deficiencies he obviously felt would not be found in his own (D, 1
Jan. 1870). From time to time, FM even indulged in reading
about spiritualism, then much in vogue. Constant brooding
over George's early death was largely responsible for this
somber interest.

     After their removal to St. Stephens Street, the senior
Maddens, sometimes accompanied by young Emily Mary, continued
a round of social activities, attending state balls, the
Queen's drawing rooms, an occasional *conversazione*, speech
days at Merchant Tailor's, Arnold's school, and dinner with
such friends as the Ravenshaws and Lady Fellows. Together or
separately they viewed pictures at the National Gallery or
the Royal Academy, paying heed to what FM considered "Pre-
Raphaelite horrors," inspected the lions guarding the base of
Nelson's monument and the unfinished Albert Memorial, observed
the reform riots in Hyde Park, joined the crowds watching
the Queen pass through Kensington Gardens with her cavalry
escort, and marveled to hear a two-headed black girl at
Willis's Rooms sing a duet very prettily. London's underground railway was still a great novelty, and in 1866 FM commented on the convenience of traveling on the Metropolitan
Line. The family continued their vacations out of town,
traveling in 1866 to Portsmouth, where FM made a nostalgic
tour of his boyhood haunts. He later had a photograph made
of the Madden house in St. Thomas Street where he had been
born and where he passed the first two decades of his life.

     With a comely daughter of marriageable age in the house-
hold, dancing parties were inevitable, and FM, imprisoned in
his study, suffered through invasions of as many as eighty
guests at such affairs. He looked painstakingly into the
pedigrees and financial prospects of suitors, and he clearly
enjoyed his role when he received a request for Emily Mary's
hand from Lieutenant-Colonel Edward Tedlie of the 60th Royal
Rifles and soon thereafter he pored over the terms of the
marriage settlement. He bore up well at the wedding in April
1870, which included a great breakfast catered for fifty
guests. He had always been especially solicitous about Emily
Mary, and he found her departure for India with her husband
only a few months later a great wrench.

Two dark events in the period just preceding the marriage
and departure led to much family tension and sorrow. First
was Fritz's loss of his post at the British Museum. He had
fully demonstrated his competence as a numismatist, yet when
he came to be involved in a questionable sale of duplicate
coins, he was obliged to resign. His father was beside himself with fury at his son's carelessness or naïvetée, and he
signaled his displeasure not only by refusing to speak to
Fritz for a considerable time but also by withdrawing his
name from the list of prospective members of the Athenaeum
Club. This attitude led to violent quarrels with Emily. Not
until 1871 was Fritz able to redeem himself in his father's
eyes by obtaining respectable employment in the newly established Kensington Museum, but in the interval he and his
growing family of young children subsisted chiefly on funds
supplied surreptitiously by his mother.

More dismaying than Fritz's problems was the discovery
late in 1868 of Emily's breast cancer. An operation was
promptly performed at home under chloroform, and the patient
made a reasonably quick recovery and seemed again to be her
cheerful self. But shortly after the wedding in April 1870,
a recurrence of the tumor was detected and the condition grew
rapidly worse. Finally, accompanied by Arnold, she journeyed
to Boulogne to consult a certain Count Matthei, but it was of
no avail. She received the final sacrament from her brother-
in-law, the Rev. Lancelot Sharpe, and died on 15 February
1873 at age fifty-nine. FM himself, for years a sufferer
from neuralgia, sinusitis, and digestive disorders, was bed-
ridden during this period. He weakened as Emily breathed her
last and his death, from what was called pleurisy, ensued in
less than a month after hers, on 8 March 1873.

.   .   .   .

The nineteenth century, and especially the first three-quar-
ters of that century, FM's life span, saw fear and depression
give way to the great acceleration in the rate of social
change and the emergence of attitudes and lines of force that
characterize what we think of as the modern era. The most
favored among European countries in the years following
Waterloo, England consolidated her empire and throve mightily.
For such reasons, we are encouraged to think of the period
as one of unequalled self-confidence, national pride, and
bursting optimism, just as we tend to associate the rise of
the middle class made prosperous by the fruits of industrial-

ism with the dominance of a code of external decorum known
as Victorian morality.

As suggested in the foregoing sketch, FM did not at every
point fit neatly into his age as it is superficially charac-
terized. He certainly did not participate in the upsurge of
optimism, but possibly his natural dourness would in any case
have inhibited any overt enthusiasm over England's imperial
triumphs and her resulting wealth and power. He was proud
of being an Englishman, but his pride often took the form of   .
arrogant derogation of foreigners close at hand, notably
Panizzi, who could scarcely be expected to understand, let
alone possess, the elements of gentlemanly conduct. On his
part, FM must have presented the image of a London gentleman
of some consequence, although of limited means, in his im-
personal manner, his attention to all the perquisites of his
position, such as attendance at court, his active membership
in the Athenaeum and the Royal Society of Literature, and
even in his rage over his son's socially unsuitable marriage.
At the same time, he was indifferent and at times hostilely
disposed toward the religious piety in which some of his contemporaries found authority for the Victorian code of personal virtue and family purity.

In his political views, he was far from sophisticated.
Quite understandably, he imbibed in Captain Madden's household in Portsmouth the family's traditional loyalty to the
sovereign and to the Tory party, and he never strayed far
from that posture. The truth is that he seldom and reluctant-
ly raised his eyes from his study table long enough to become
informed about the issues of the day. In his Diary and correspondence there is mention, for the most part, of only
those political figures and officers of state who had a di-
rect connection with the Museum. Occasionally, however, he
complained about "dirty Whig radicals," and he contemptuously
ascribed the reversal of a sentence passed on Daniel O'Con-
nell in 1844 to Whig lords. On the other hand, his reading
of Mrs. Trollope's *Michael Armstrong* seems to have forced
from him the admission that mill-owners might be guilty of
atrocities against their employees and that they might be
suspected of opposing corn laws for the sake of insuring
cheap labor (D, 9 Sept. 1842). In later life, he expressed
dislike of Gladstone and Disraeli, the former because he felt
him to have been responsible for his being granted only a
small pension, and the latter because FM took offense at the
Prime Minister's behavior toward him during a visit to the
Museum. His comment in 1860 to the effect that he hated Whigs
and their pretended liberalism and their cold-blooded, mean,
and fallacious policies which led the government to ruin by

playing into the hands of the French grew more from pique
with certain members of the Museum Trustees than from any
firm knowledge of politics.   Perhaps the most succinct statement of his credo appears in a letter he wrote in 1867 to
decline membership in the Marylebone Constitutional Union:
"I have always avoided political parties because of my official position ... but ... I had little to be thankful for
from either Whigs or Tories, and less from the Church.   I
detest democracy and mob rule" (D, 27 Dec. 1867).

FM's mistrust of democracy manifested itself early.   When,
at the age of eighteen, he and two friends were set upon by
drunken roughnecks, he fulminated against "the boasted liberty and Jacquancy England allows to its lower classes.... If
this be liberty, give me despotism!" (D, 23 Aug. 1819).
Nearly half a century later, a brickbat was thrown at him
while he was walking his dog Fan, giving rise to much the
same kind of rhetoric: "This is one of the effects of raising
the lower classes and giving them holidays" (D, 18 Aug. 1867).
Although he seemed oblivious to the Reform Riots of 1831, including the violence at Bristol that autumn, he could scarcely maintain his aloofness when the Chartist agitation was
centered in London in 1848.   In that year, in fact, he was
twice sworn in as a special constable, somewhat to his amuse-
ment, one of the steps taken by the Wellington government,
along with the dispatch of troops, to protect the Museum from
possible assault by mobs gathering nearby.   In 1866, after
viewing a Reform meeting with his son Arnold, he was moved to
remark that the rabble turned the whole affair into a joke
and that he wished a body of troops had been present to fire
point-blank into the scoundrels: "Reform indeed!" (D, 23 July
1866).   Even so, there were limits even to FM's insensitivi-
ty, as suggested in the indignation he felt on hearing a
clergyman sermonize about the great potato famine as a just
punishment of the Irish for their Roman Catholicism: "Such
monstrous and infamous doctrine!" (D, 28 Sept. 1849).

Only sporadically did world events attract his interest,
even foreign wars directly affecting the nation.   In 1854,
however, he noted the fall of Sebastopol and expressed a kind
of unfocused disgust with the Crimean War.   With the greater
leisure that came with retirement, concern with the outside
world increased somewhat.   During the Franco-Prussian War he
began taking in two daily newspapers in order to follow the
progress of hostilities.   In his Diary, he noted the capture
of Napoleon III with MacMahon's army at Sedan, the sad burning of the library at Strasbourg, and the capitulation of
Paris late in January 1871.

   At no time during his life was FM able to feel financially
comfortable. In part because of a need to maintain a standard of living commensurate with what he regarded as his social position, he was at times, in fact, hard pressed. Yet
only in his years as a widower could he have been considered
guilty of mild personal extravagance in keeping a horse and
cab and making occasional small gifts of money to his mistresses. In 1835, he commented bitterly that his money simply melted away and that he was "as poor as a rat" (D, 18
Sept. 1835). Salaries at the Museum were, of course, low,
as shown in the fact that Dr. Robinson withheld his approval
of FM's marriage to his daughter until he was advanced to
the position of Keeper of Manuscripts at an annual salary of
six hundred pounds. FM's honoraria were of occasional assistance, but clearly he could meet his obligations regularly
chiefly because he was the recipient of a few small inheritances. His share of his father's estate, less than eight
hundred pounds, helped sustain him in the 1830's, and the
Madden household enjoyed a small subsidy, one hundred pounds
annually besides an initial sum of one thousand pounds, as the
result of his marriage settlement with Dr. Robinson. After
1847, however, the annual subsidy was withdrawn by Dr. Robinson (D, 29 Dec. 1847). Upon the death of Emily's parents in
1848 and 1856, the couple inherited some small pieces of real
estate, most of which were rather soon sold. FM sometimes
allowed himself to be optimistic about much more substantial
inheritances from distant relatives, such as the Rev. David
Powell, who died in 1848 leaving some thirty thousand pounds
to St. George's Hospital, but these hopes failed to material-
ize. As already indicated, however, he received a share
amounting to several hundred pounds from his brother Henry's
twenty-thousand-pound estate in 1863 (D, 26 Nov. 1863; 29
Nov. 1864).
   On several occasions after a small windfall, FM invested
in the stock of such companies as the Cambridge and Lincoln
Railway, only to be obliged by his financial needs to sell
out, usually at a loss (D, 10 June, 31 Dec. 1845). He obviously lacked Henry Madden's acumen in managing investments.
For many years the 31 December entries in his Diary contain
outbursts such as "Oh money, money! What a curse thou art!"
(D, 31 Dec. 1852). Yet to reduce Lady Madden's domestic
staff or to curtail the education of his children would have
been an intolerable alternative. FM's retirement on a pension of six hundred pounds per year, two-thirds of his high-
est salary and considerably inferior to the pension granted
Panizzi, was possibly less difficult than might have been
expected (D, 3 Apr. 1865; 23 July 1866), and he contrived to

meet Arnold's expenses at his university and to launch Emily Mary into society.

Up to the final months of his life, FM continued his omnivorous reading. His closest attention was always reserved for such works as Count Montalembert's *Monks of the West* and Morris's *Early English Alliterative Poems*, with which he was occupied almost to the last day, yet he also read and commented about a wide range of current publications, including much fiction, some biography, and a little poetry. In his youth, he set down his pompous pronouncements about Scott's *The Abbot*, *The Monastery*, *Ivanhoe*, and *Kenilworth*, to several of which he returned fifty years later with pleasure and respect. He began Dickens in 1846 with the remark that *The Cricket on the Hearth* was too popular or low, and he applied similar epithets to *Little Dorrit*, *Pictures of Italy*, *David Copperfield*, *Bleak House*, and others of the novels as the years passed. In 1872, he went so far as to call *Edwin Drood* "rubbish." The fact remains, however, that he read a fair number of Dickens's works, that he attended one of the author's dramatic performances, and that he responded to news of his sudden death in June 1870 with an expression of genuine regret. Indeed, to no other novelist did he devote so many Diary entries.

Charlotte Brontë's *Jane Eyre* appealed to him as a work of some intellect, but he found himself unable to sympathize with either heroine or hero. His introduction to Thackeray began in 1849 with *Vanity Fair*, parts of which he thought very affecting. Some years later he read *Henry Esmond* and *The Newcomes* with little enthusiasm, and in 1869, when he returned to *Vanity Fair*, he declared it to be the best of Thackeray, "which isn't saying much" (D, 25 Aug. 1869). Rather surprisingly, George Eliot struck him as one "ignorant of human nature" and "dull," on the basis of *The Mill on the Floss* and *Felix Holt*. The novels of Anthony Trollope, on the other hand, especially *Dr. Thorne*, he considered well written and absorbing. He read at least nine of Bulwer-Lytton's books in the face of what he regarded as ignorance of medieval times and a tendency toward self-glorification. On finishing Harriet Beecher Stowe's *Uncle Tom's Cabin* in 1852, he forgot his usual disdain for American writing in confessing that it moved him to tears (D, 3 Oct. 1852).

FM was stubbornly unimpressed by the great essayists and biographers of the period. He spoke of Macaulay as "truculent" and "overpraised," even though he considered that the Milton essay was "fair" and the treatment of Addison "admirable." Carlyle, however, never failed to arouse indignation because of his "detestable style," "corruption of the English

language," and "empty bombast" in *Heroes and Hero-Worship*,
The History of Frederick the Great, and *The French Revolution*
(D, 11 July, 18, 24 Sept. 1854; 24 Feb. 1861; 15 Jan., 19
Feb. 1862; 1 Oct. 1870). Here is another instance of FM's
persisting in the reading of an author for whom he professed
disapproval or contempt. The first volume of Coleridge's
Table Talk, which he read because he had heard much about the
author's brilliant conversation, was a disappointment. Although conceding that Coleridge was deeply read, he dismissed
his opinions as "visionary," "dogmatical," or "trivial." An
early installment of Matthew Arnold's "Literature and Dogma"
in *Cornhill Magazine* attracted his attention, but he claimed
to be unable to follow the argument, even though he approved
of Arnold's ridicule of absurd bishops.

The poetry of the romantics touched FM very glancingly indeed, and perhaps his assertion "I detest modern poetry,"
made in the context of his severe strictures on Coleridge's
poetic "nonsense," should be taken as more than an outburst
of momentary irritation (D, 14 Oct. 1845). Yet he believed
that Macaulay's *Lays of Ancient Rome* showed great poetic power despite license in language, and he concluded, on reading
Alastor and *The Revolt of Islam*, that Shelley, albeit a visionary, was much superior to Southey. Landor likewise he
regarded as better than Southey. He was proof against the
charms of Tennyson, including what he read of *The Idylls of
the King*, and noted churlishly that "people are fools to talk
in raptures of his poetry" (D, 19 June 1868; 21 Oct., 30 Nov.
1871).

In addition to the writers just mentioned, FM read George
Borrow, Wilkie Collins, Benjamin Disraeli, Charles Kingsley,
Dante Gabriel Rossetti, James Fenimore Cooper, and John Ruskin, to say nothing of minor figures, such as the popular
historian Agnes Strickland and the novelist Marie Louise de
la Ramée (Ouida). His preference for fiction is scarcely
surprising in that age of novel-reading. Never, on the other
hand, did he immerse himself in the flood of third-rate ro-
mantic fiction of the times as no less a personage than T.B.
Macaulay is said by his sister to have done during his early
life.

With some authors, including Scott, Thackeray, the Dis-
raelis, father and son, Carlyle, and Ruskin, FM had some
slight personal acquaintance through correspondence or encounters in the Museum. At a dinner of the Literary Fund in
1864, which he attended with Emily and Emily Mary, he heard
Trollope and Thackeray return thanks on behalf of English
authors to the Prince of Wales and Lord Russell for the laud-
atory addresses by those dignitaries. Judging from his ex-

pressed reactions to experiences such as this one as well as
to his reading, we may see that FM's appreciation of many
writers tended to be stifled by a degree of envy of the fame
and adulation, to say nothing of the wealth, they had won.
At times, the Diary entries tempt one to feel that he persisted in his reading of Carlyle and others less out of
pleasure than from a compulsion to indulge in lofty deprecia-
tion. When he was dealing with medieval literature, his critical faculties were much freer. A case in point is his recognition of the beauty of the great fourteenth-century dream-
vision, *Pearl*, and the fine alliterative romance, *Morte Ar-
thure*. Although he admired Robert Mannyng of Brunne's *Hand-
lyng Synne*, he judiciously assigned it a lower place than
either of those poems (FM's note to Warton's *History of English Poetry*, ed. Hazlitt, II, 88-89, fn. 6).

Taken by themselves, FM's often crabbed *obiter dicta* on
nineteenth-century literary works now seen to possess great
beauty and merit may strike the modern reader as the product
of a limited, nonliterary mind. Yet many if not most of his
adverse opinions, such as his remarks about Charlotte Brontë,
were also those of highly regarded reviewers and were certainly widespread among FM's friends. Especially his coolness toward Tennyson and Landor and his hostility toward Pre-
Raphaelite art could not have seemed eccentric. In fact, in
those areas in which he never considered himself an expert,
he could at worst be called a conservative.

The present-day reader of the Diary could also be easily
led to think of FM as strangely oblivious to the momentous
mid-century advances in scientific thought, for he can find
therein no notice of Darwin's *Origin of Species* (1859) or of
the Huxley-Wilberforce debate at Oxford in late June 1860.
Conceivably, FM's careful reading in 1856 of *Vestiges of the
Natural History of Creation*, anonymously published in 1844
but later revealed to be by Huxley's friend, Robert Chambers,
had the effect of inuring him to the later and now much
better-known attacks of science on the orthodox story of creation. If so, Chambers's book did for FM the service pre-
dicted for it by Darwin—namely, removing prejudice and preparing the ground for "analogous views." In any case, FM's
terse comment about Chambers suggests his readiness for the
modern world in this respect: "I cannot help fearing the
author of *Vestiges of Creation* is right" (D, 18 Apr. 1856).
He could also admit that Paley, whose *Natural Theology* and
View of the Evidences of Christianity he had read in his
youth, had been superseded. Even Du Chaillu's startling theory about the descent of the white race from chimpanzees and
the black race from gorillas he was able to take in stride
(D, 8, 28 Apr. 1821; 17 June 1867).

The devastating blow dealt by his son's death in 1865 had
the effect of turning FM's thoughts toward the immortality
of the soul. During the sharpest period of his grief, he
looked in Huxley's work for information about the human brain,
Archbishop Sumner's theory of the progressive improvement of
man's reason, and Sir Richard Owen's views on the possibility
of an extra-mundane agency. At the same time, he studied Sir
Charles Lyell's latest book, *The Antiquity of Man*, confessing
he found it hard going. His grief even led him to succumb to
the rage for spiritualism, although in his comments on sé-
ances he attended and communication with the dead his charac-
teristic skepticism wins through. All available evidence
suggests that FM had at least the degree of concern with science and its implications and also with the spiritualist
movement that one could impute to his educated contemporaries.

Apart from the field of scholarship which he had made his
own, FM could scarcely have appealed to friends and associates as creative or daring. Although exceptionally well-read
in most branches of the literature of the day, he was not
fitted by nature to heed and appreciate the new voices. One
would not expect from him the kind of original and perceptive
remarks made about Keats by another diarist, Henry Crabb
Robinson, for example. Yet he was intellectually flexible
enough to absorb and approve of the new scientific thought,
or of as much of it as he had read. In the areas of politics
and world affairs, in which he was far less well informed,
his views, on the whole, were predictable stereotypes. His
old-fashioned Toryism was only slightly touched by the social
and economic upheavals of the middle decades of the century.

The Diary itself offers further insights into FM's charac-
ter. For this fifty-three-year, four-million-word production
is far more than a chronology of experiences and events, despite the youthful Frederic's initial announcement of the
policy he would follow: "I have only aimed at what its title
purports--that of a Diary or daily *Notebook* of my actions.
I have not, like most journalists, launched into a tedious
description of my feelings on any occasion" (D, flyleaf,
1818). At the conclusion of his first year, he leafed
through his entries and decided that he would thenceforth
record his "actions" in less circumstantial detail. But very
little if any diminution is to be noted in subsequent years.
Moreover, the space occupied by each day, running from a few
lines to as many as five pages, is devoted not simply to objective accounts of actions but also to outlines of and comments about his reading and the not seldom anguished expression of his private emotions, precisely the sort of revelations he had initially decided to exclude.

Especially in his birthday entries, 16 February, was FM prone to lay bare his inner state, a practice he tended to maintain throughout the Diary. Typically, he indulged in self-pitying remarks about the passage of time: "I am fifty, half a century. Ens entium! Miserere mei!" (D, 16 Feb. 1851). New Year's Eve was another occasion that prompted gloomy remarks about his weariness with "this fagging, sedentary life," the "infirm" state of his health, vexation over money matters, a desire to get away from the Museum, his "house of bondage," concern over his slow progress with scholarly work, or worry over his children's future. He memorialized the anniversary of George's death just as he had for years that of Mary, and, as suggested above, he was unable to allude to Panizzi without disparagement. His resentment of his colleague was stirred up both by major issues, such as the battle over the Grenville Library, and by minor annoyances, as on the occasion when Panizzi sought to invoke an old rule that would have prevented him from keeping a dog in his Museum apartment. A great fulmination was also forthcoming when, well after retirement, Panizzi was honored with a Knight-Companionship of the Bath. As late as 1872, FM seethed at the mere thought of Panizzi, writing at that time, "Daily, hourly, I curse him!" (D, 1 Sept. 1872).

Against these explosions of wrath and extreme irritability, arising generally out of wounded dignity, one may set the many outpourings of FM's warmer nature. In his youthful rhapsodies over Mary Hayton, appearing in the Diary and with almost unbearable extravagance in the "Private Memoirs," of which only a fragment is known to survive, in his quieter affirmations of his love for his second wife and his agonies over her terminal illness, and in his devotion to his children, which not even his extreme displeasure with Fritz can efface, one can sense the depths of his humanity. FM was not always well-disposed toward all his siblings, but we find him on occasion remitting funds he could not easily spare to his eccentric maiden sister Maria and in her old age he entertained her in his house, although in a gingerly fashion. He was always affectionate toward Emma, the youngest, who died in 1844 after several years of mental illness. He made her his sole heir while he was a widower, and it is worth noting that a falling out with his bachelor brother Henry was caused by what he considered Henry's unfeeling and ungenerous conduct toward Emma.

Another rather appealing facet of FM's nature was, despite his unhappy associations with horses, his lifelong fondness for pet animals, beginning with a beautiful tame deer brought home to Portsmouth from Vera Cruz by his sailor brother

Charles. In London, a pampered dog or cat was generally a
fixture of the household. In fact, a "French" tom-cat named
Mouton, given to FM by a bookseller in 1854, was the innocent
cause of increased exasperation with Panizzi when he was shut
up for two days or so in the latter's basement not, in FM's
opinion, by accident. The cat came home, however, before
anyone claimed the twenty-shilling reward. Despite the min-
istrations of an experienced zoo-keeper and veterinarian,
Mouton died five years later, whereupon FM had him stuffed
and set up in the dining room and, as a further memorial,
published an epitaph to him in French in *Notes & Queries*
(Bib. No. 147). Mouton's successor, also a "French" cat,
called Memel, died of phthisis, and thereafter dogs were pre-
ferred. The first of these, Fido, a Blenheim Spaniel, was
the animal that aroused Panizzi's anger and prompted a quar-
rel, one of the few altercations with his rival in which FM
was victorious. Fido's demise is announced in the Diary as
follows: "Dies nefastus! I loved him next to wife and children." He was buried under a lilac bush on the Museum premises (D, 28 Oct., 4, 7, 15 Nov. 1861; 7, 8 June 1864). The
last pet, another Blenheim, named Lady Fan, was still living,
though ill and under medical treatment, at the time of the
last Diary entry in 1872. Despite the largely despairing
nature of his Christmas entry in 1869, FM gives us a pleasant
vignette of himself working in his study "with Fan as usual
on my lap."
    There is, moreover, FM's unexpectedly gamesome nature to
be taken into account. His early zeal as a ballroom dancer
waned somewhat, yet he continued to attend dances well into
middle life, and not entirely to please Emily. He was forty-
three when, chancing to witness his sisters-in-law at a dancing lesson with Miss Finney, he seized the opportunity of
learning the steps and figures of the polka, which six months
earlier he had derided on seeing it performed at the Ravenshaws'. As a conscientious father, he showed slides on his
magic lantern at juvenile birthday parties, and he once sent
to a child a valentine signed with the name of the current
family cat. Sometimes, on vacations, he played the games of
his youth with the children and also the Robinson sisters,
such as Consequences, Forfeits, Pope Joan, Vingt-et-un, Whist,
Cribbage, Besique, and Tactics. Chess, however, he took seriously and for a time was a member of a chess club in Bed-
ford Street. After the 1830's, he had little free time for
the game, but his knowledge of chess and its history stood
him in good stead when an Edinburgh dealer in 1831 sold to
the Museum a trove of eighty-two ancient chess pieces that
had been discovered in the sand on the Island of Lewis, off

Scotland. He examined these pieces, carved from walrus ivo-
ry, with Sir Walter Scott, during the latter's visit to the
Museum in October 1831.

Although he attended plays with parents and friends in
Portsmouth and later in London went occasionally to the theater, FM was never an aficionado, as was Henry Crabb Robinson.
He saw Edmund Kean in a play called *Brutus* in 1819 and also
the "celebrated Miss Clara Fisher" and her two sisters. He
differed from most in failing to be moved by Edwin Forrest's
King Lear in 1836. Possibly at his bidding, George and Fritz
attended a performance of Charles Kean's *Hamlet* years later
but their reactions are not recorded; FM himself thought well
of the same actor's *Louis XI* soon thereafter. He and Emily
were both pleased with Lydia Thompson's dancing and acting in
A Day in Paris and *Magic Toys*, which they saw at St. James's
Theatre, but Edward Sothern as Lord Dundreary in *Our American
Cousin* struck FM, at least, as poor. Especially during the
years following Mary's death and before his remarriage, FM
was amused by the pantomimes and similar performances playing
in the London theaters, often attending in the company of a
current mistress. His first opera, *La Traviata*, he saw with
Henry and declared himself much pleased, and in 1852 he sat
in a private box with some ladies to hear a concert by Paga-
nini. Music interested him only slightly, however, and such
events were rare in his life until Emily set out to provide
some musical sophistication for their daughter. For example,
the three of them heard Patti sing *La Sonnambula*.

Already noted is FM's frequent appearance at court func-
tions and other affairs which permitted him to mingle with
the upper classes. He and Emily were regular attendants at
the Queen's annual balls until their names were removed from
the invitation list. But FM was always equally fond of spectacles and amusements open to the general public, making sure
that his children saw the fireworks displays, the gas illumi-
nations, and the military parades and exercises marking occasions such as a visit of the Princess Alexandra in 1864.
Returning from the theater on the evening of 15 October 1834,
he noticed that the sky was lurid from a great conflagration.
Because he was tired and had work to finish in his study, he
did not, to his later regret, set out then for the scene of
the fire, which virtually destroyed the Palace of Westminster.
In the 1840's, he followed closely and critically the con-
struction of the new palace, that is, the Parliament Building, with particular reference to the interior decorations.
He kept abreast of other large building projects in the city,
visiting by private ticket a model of Nelson's Monument in
1839; in 1860 he walked out with the children to see the new

Westminster Bridge; and not long thereafter he and Jamie inspected the Blackfriar's Railway Bridge. Ostensibly as another treat for Jamie, he went to Cremorne to watch a hot-air
balloon ascension by a French aeronaut in the summer of 1864.

FM was capable of disapproving strongly of innovations,
such as the "beastly envelopes and sticking stamps" issued
by the post office in 1840. On the other hand, he welcomed
the coming of rail travel and commented wonderingly on the
speed of trains and on passenger fares. On a trip to Cambridge in 1843, he noted how the coach was lifted off the
rails at Harlon and drawn from that point by horses. He was
likewise well disposed toward the underground rail system in
London, first traveling by that means in 1863. Evidently the
speed and convenience of this mode of getting about London
compensated for the dense smoke and soot about which other
travelers complained.

The Great Exhibition of 1851 was for him almost endlessly
interesting. Early that year, he took the boys to Hyde Park
to marvel at the daring iron frame of the "glass house," and
four days before the gala opening on 1 May, he walked around
the completed Crystal Palace, one in a crowd of gaping spec-
tators. Although he did not attend the opening celebration
in the Palace, as did the Robinsons, he and George watched
the Queen, the Lord Mayor, and the Sheriffs parade along Rot-
ten Row that day with their retinues. But on 5 May, he spent
several gratifying hours at the Exhibition and shortly thereafter made a series of shorter visits with various family
members. Even at the end of the year, when the Crystal Palace had been dismantled and moved to Sydenham Hill, the Maddens now and then found their way to this suburban site where
they saw medieval exhibits, watched Blondin perform on the
tightrope, and attended a Foresters' Fête.

A lesser place of resort was the Egyptian Hall, which fea-
tured exotic spectacles, such as a group of American Indians
in native regalia. At other halls, pitiful human freaks were
on show, like the two-headed black girl mentioned above. FM
was much amused by a "climbing boy" at the Olympic Theater
and an enormously fat eleven-year-old lad at the Royal Society,
and he found time to wonder at a "double-visioned" Scotch
boy, performing fish, and the embalmed corpse of Julia Pas-
trama and child. Accompanied by Emily, he looked over the
plate, diamonds, and furniture of the "mysterious Mrs.
Thwaite," and he enjoyed seeing General Tom Thumb and his
company of midgets on several occasions. With the Robinson
ladies, he visited Madame Tussaud's waxworks, concluding that
the best exhibits there were of persons in low life, such as
Hare and Hobbit.

The account of FM's lighter amusements would be incomplete
without attention to his fondness for zoological gardens and
other parks. In 1841, he attended what was billed as the
last evening at Vauxhall Gardens before its destruction, noting that this once extremely popular resort was thinly pa-
tronized. Early in his London residence, he began visiting
the Zoological Gardens, for which he held an admission ticket
many years. During the 1830's in particular, he was accus-
tomed to stroll there, often with Julia, Emma, or one of his
other mistresses. On one such walk, he was greatly diverted
when an elephant, which had been allowed out of his enclo-
sure, uprooted park trees. In later years, he rather often
took his children there to see the hippos and other speci-
mens. Once he commented that only in the Zoological Gardens
did he feel that he could "indulge his spleen without notice"
(D, 21 May 1832). Hyde Park and Kensington Gardens were also
pleasing to him, and beginning in the 1860's, he more and
more walked in horticultural gardens, such as Kew.

Here, then, stands Frederic Madden, about whom, thanks to
a wealth of documentation, we are able to learn more of what
is important to know than we can about almost any other person of similar consequence in the century. Even reliable
visual impressions are possible, not simply from the British
Library portrait representing the subject at age thirty-six
and the several *carte-de-visite* photographs that have been
preserved, but also from drawings and verbal descriptions.
The portrait tells us at once that he bore no resemblance to
William Langland's iconographical image of Ira, depicted as
long and cadaverous, with contorted features and white eyes,
although Panizzi's biographer may lead one to expect such an
apparition by his tendency to characterize FM as "fierce and
implacable," "furious," "complaining," "aggrieved," "fiery,"
"redoubtable," and even "skinny" (Bib. No. 288). The 1837
portrait shows us rather a dark-haired, bespectacled man with
elongated side-burns, whose expression suggests mildness and
repose. The expression may be owing to the artist, of
course, but the fine eyes, somewhat aquiline nose, and strong
chin seem to have been taken from life accurately enough.

Only a year earlier, in May 1836, Robert Curzon in a letter quoted by Munby (Bib. No. 289) described FM in vivid
terms: "... a young man with large whiskers & a smart stick &
a waistcoat, & does not look half as much of a Bibliomaniac
as you do, but notwithstanding his appearance is uncommon sly
and knows more about the matter than anyone whom I have seen,
except Angelo Mai [Vatican librarian] perhaps." This dandi-
fied impression is borne out by an 1833 watercolor in Munby's
possession, showing the side whiskers, eye-glass, and stick
in profile.

FM's French visa, dated 24 July 1838, contains a brief description that accords well with the pictures: "cheveux, bruns; Front, onde; Sourcils, bruns; Yeux, bruns; Nez, moyen; Menton, ronde" (D, 30 July 1838). That he was by no means a tall man is suggested by an early sketch he made of himself standing beside Sir Henry Ellis, known to have been short and fat (D, 12 Apr. 1824). That he remained slender in later life is clear since at age fifty-four he weighed ten stone, thirteen pounds (153 pounds), according to a railway station scales. On that same day, Emily was found to weigh nine stone, thirteen pounds (138 pounds) (D, 13 Sept. 1855). The rather stately photographs taken some years later show FM to be white-haired and bearded, but still in his sixties he was erect and slim of figure. On the whole, we may picture him throughout life as a rather good-looking, medium-size man, carefully dressed and formal in manner. In contrast, Panizzi, although he did not deserve the epithet of "gorilla" applied to him by FM (D, 22 Jan. 1862), was a tall man, heavy in body and in features. If FM seemed formidable to associates and contemporaries, as to some he certainly did, it was not by virtue of his mere physical presence but rather because of his alertness to any threat to his dignity and his readiness to express his displeasure.

A personality so defensive and lofty is not an asset whatever one's position in life. But in an important member of an institution consisting of persons of a certain amount of education and social standing, it would inevitably be a handicap. On the other hand, FM won and for forty years sustained his position in the British Museum by his dedication to duty and his superb scholarship. The luster of his achievements in this area, including his restoration of the Cottonian Library, repaid the Museum and the nation many times over.

PART TWO

BIBLIOGRAPHY A

Madden's Publications

1. "Antiquities," *PPSGLSR*, No. 1 (20 June 1822), 5-8.

   Signed "Z" (see Abbreviations). A letter congratulating the editor on the liberal nature of his new journal. FM is not, he states, one of those pedants who retire into their corners crying "Procul o profani!" D, 31 May, 4, 14, 20, 29 June, 4, 5 July 1822.

2. "Alice and Richard, A Local Tale," *PPGLSR*, No. 2 (18 July 1822), 17-23.

   Signed "O.B." (see Abbreviations). A short tragedy based in part on Portsmouth historical records first called to FM's attention by Lake Allen. Although FM acknowledged that fiction was "not a style fate adapted to my taste," he initially submitted the story to Colbourne's *New Monthly Magazine*, and only after its rejection did he offer it to D.B. Price, editor of *PPGLSR*. In 1840, Price reprinted the tale in his *Portsmouth Tracts*, No. 1. D, 30 Nov., 1, 9, 29 Dec. 1821; 31 May, 4, 14, etc. June, 19 July 1822; 4 July 1840.

3. "On the Origin and Progress of Fairs," *PPGLSR*, No. 5 (17 Oct. 1822), 98-107.

   Signed "Philagoras" (see Abbreviations). A short historical essay tracing fairs from Roman into early English times.

4. "Warblington Castle and Church," *PPGLSR*, No. 8 (16 Jan. 1823), 161-72, continued in No. 9 (20 Feb. 1823), 185-94.

   Signed "Z" (see Abbreviations). A serious piece of historical research evidently going well beyond the existing histories of Hampshire. Part I traces the successive

holders of the manor of Warblington, and Part II provides
a careful description of the ruins of the castle and also
of the church. In the copy of this journal held by the
BL are to be seen FM's later marginal corrections and additions to his Warblington article. D, 17 Oct. 1822; 16
Jan. 1823.

5. *C. Suetonii Quintilli Opera Omnia ex Editione Baumgarten-*
    Crusii cum Notis et Interpretatione in usum Delphini
    variis lectionibus Notis Variorum recensu editionum et
    codicum et Indice Locupletissimo accurate Recensita, 3
    vols., London: A.J. Valpy, 1826.

    While searching for a means of eking out his meager re-
    muneration as a copyist, FM obtained late in 1824 a com-
    mission from the publisher Valpy to add variorum notes to
    a new printing of a standard edition of Suetonius. FM's
    name does not appear in the book, published early in
    1826, but his journal entries testify to the great amount
    of time and effort he devoted to the project. Valpy paid
    him forty-five pounds for his pains. D, 28 Aug., 12
    Oct., 1, 28 Nov. 1824; 6, 31 Jan., 7, 28 Mar., 11, 18
    Apr., 22 May, 21 Aug., 3 Sept., 3 Oct., 1, 22, 27, 30
    Dec. 1825; 7 Apr. 1826.

6. [Vindications of the late Joseph Ritson], *Gent. Mag.*,
    CXXXVII (June 1825), 486-88.

    Signed "Ritsonianus" (see Abbreviations). In this un-
    titled communication, FM comments on the 1824 edition of
    Warton's *History of English Poetry* (see Bib. No. 317) in
    which the editor, Richard Price, expresses resentment
    about Ritson's criticism of Warton for his many inaccura-
    cies. FM, who was to supply many corrections and addi-
    tions to the 1840 and 1871 editions of the same work (see
    Bib. Nos. 72, 154), allies himself with Ritson, whom he
    considered a great proponent of responsible editorial
    scholarship. D, 4 July 1825.

7. *The Ancient English Romance of Havelok the Dane; Accom-*
    panied by the French Text; with an Introduction, Notes,
    and Glossary, by Frederick Madden, Esq., F.A.S.,
    F.R.S.L., Sub-Keeper of the MSS. in the British Museum,
    Roxburghe Club, London: W. Nicol, Shakspeare Press, 1828.

    As indicated in the biographical sketch (Part One), FM's
    discovery in 1825 of the long-mislaid MS. (Bodleian MS.
    Laud Misc. 108) containing *Havelok* and the appearance

years later of his edition of that work may be said to
have launched his career. Two early commentators questioned FM's interpretation of a few words in *Havelok* and
even his command of Middle English in general. To the
first of these critics, S.W. Singer, he published a tell-
ing response (see Bib. Nos. 304, 9), but he felt
obliged to take more seriously the remarks of the second, J.M. Kemble (see Bib. No. 283), since he knew them
to be based on a sound knowledge of the then-new work
on Germanic philology. Indeed, he was moved to confide
in his Diary that Kemble aroused him to a sense of what
was due his recently begun edition of Layamon. It
should be noted, however, that W.W. Skeat, in his reedition of the romance for the Early English Text Society
forty years later, affirmed enthusiastically the cor-
rectness of FM's palaeographical work and much of his
critical apparatus. D, 12 Aug., 1 Oct. 1825; 17 Jan.,
29 July, 14 Aug., 19 Dec. 1826; 6-8 Mar., 18, 28 Sept.,
16 Nov. 1827; 12 Jan., 6, etc. Feb., 10 Mar., 2 Apr.,
3 May, 7 Aug., 14 Sept., 4, 16 Oct., etc. 1828.

8. Nicholas Harris Nicolas, *The Siege of Carlaverock in the
XXVIIIth Edward I, A.D. MCCC*, reviewed by FM, *Gent.
Mag.*, CXLIII (May 1828), 419-21, CXLIV (Dec. 1828), 493-
95.

   Signed "A Clerk of Oxenforde" (see Abbreviations). The
   author, Nicolas, and the historian, S.R. Meyrick, re-
   plied to the "Clerk of Oxenforde" in *Gent. Mag.*, CXLV
   (Jan. 1829), 25-28. D, 7 Jan. 1829.

9. *Examination of the "Remarks on the Glossary to the Antient Metrical Romance of Havelok the Dane, ... by S.W.
Singer,"* addressed to Henry Petrie, Esq., by the Editor
of *Havelok*, London: W. Nicol, 1829.

   FM's formal rebuttal of the sixteen-page critique of
   Havelok published by Singer in 1829 (see Bib. No. 304).
   D, 7 Jan., 4 Sept. 1829.

10. "Ancient Norman French Poem on the Erection of the Walls
of New Ross in Ireland, A.D. 1265," *Arch.*, XXII (1829-
30), 307-22.

   "Communicated by Frederic Madden, Esq., F.S.A., in a
   Letter to Henry Ellis, Esq., F.R.S., Secretary." Read
   22 Jan. 1829. D, 31 Mar. 1829.

11. "Old English Poem on the Siege of Rouen, 1418," *Arch.*,
     XXII (1829-30), 350-98.

     "Communicated by Frederic Madden, Esq., F.S.A., in a
     Letter to Henry Ellis, Esq., F.R.S., Secretary." Read
     2 Apr. 1829.

12. "Petition of Richard Troughton, Bailiff of South Witham,
     Lincolnshire, to the Privy Council in the Reign of Queen
     Mary," *Arch.*, XXIII (1830-31), 18-49.

     "Communicated by Frederic Madden, Esq., F.S.A., in a
     Letter to Thomas Amyot, Esq., F.R.S., Treasurer." Read
     3 Dec. 1829.

13. [Seal of Evesham Abbey], *Gent. Mag.*, CXLVII (Apr. 1830),
     310-11.

     Signed "Frederick Madden." A short reply by Joseph
     Hunter appears in *Gent. Mag.*, CXLVII (May 1830), 392.

14. [Another Impression of the Seal of Evesham Abbey], *Gent.
     Mag.*, CXLVIII (July 1830), 2.

15. [Black Book of Winchester], *Gent. Mag.*, new ser., C
     (Dec. 1830), 401-02.

     Signed "Hantoniensis" (see Abbreviations).

16. "Regalia of Scotland," *Gent. Mag.*, new ser., C (Dec.
     1830), 483-85.

     Signed "Fred. Madden." D, 12 Dec. 1830.

17. [Transcript of Archbishop Arundel's Letter to Henry IV],
     included in Thomas Amyot, "A Reply to Mr. Tytler's His-
     torical Remarks on the Death of Richard the Second,"
     Arch., XXIII (1830-31), 297-98.

     "Communicated by Thomas Amyot, Esq., F.R.S., Treasurer,
     to Henry Ellis, Esq., F.R.S., Secretary." Paper read
     9 Dec. 1830. Amyot states that the Arundel letter was
     transcribed "by my friend Mr. Madden."

18. [On Entries Touching on the Birth of King Edward's
     Children], *Gent. Mag.*, new ser., CI (Jan. 1831), 23-25.
     Signed "F.M."

19. "Account of King Henry the Eighth's Entry into Lincoln
     in 1541," *Arch.*, XXIII (1830-31), 334-38.

"Communicated in a letter to Henry Ellis, Esq., F.R.S., Secretary, from Frederic Madden, Esq., F.S.A." Read 20 Jan. 1831. A notice of this paper appears in *Gent. Mag.*, new ser., CI (Jan. 1831), 75.

20. "Narrative of the Visit of the Duke de Nájera to England, in the year 1543-4; written by his Secretary, Pedro de Gante," *Arch.*, XXIII (1830-31), 344-57.

    "Communicated in a Letter to Hudson Gurney, Esq., M.P., Vice President S.A. by Frederic Madden, Esq., F.S.A." Read 27 Jan. 1831.

21. [Game Played by Boys in England], *Gent. Mag.*, new ser., CI (Feb. 1831), 123-24.

    Signed "Bucca" (see Abbreviations). A comment on E.H. Barker's "Micatio Digitorum," *Gent. Mag.*, new ser., C (Dec. 1830), 508-09.

22. Nicholas Harris Nicolas, *Privy Purse Expenses of Elizabeth of York: Wardrobe Accounts of Edward the Fourth*, reviewed in *Gent. Mag.*, new ser., CI (Feb. 1831), 153-56.

    This unsigned review is conjecturally assigned to FM chiefly because of his interest in such historical data, as reflected in his own edition of the *Privy Purse Expenses of the Princess Mary* (see Bib. No. 26).

23. "Description of the Matrix of the Seal of Southwick Priory in Hampshire," *Arch.*, XXIII (1830-31), 374-79.

    "Communicated in a Letter to Thomas Amyot, Esq., Treasurer, from Frederic Madden, Esq., F.S.A." Paper read 24 Mar. 1831. A notice of this paper appears in *Gent. Mag.*, new ser., CI (Mar. 1831), 254. D, 2, 8 Apr. 1831.

24. "St. Katherine's Hospital Near the Tower," *Gent. Mag.*, new ser., CI (May 1831), 391-92.

    Signed "K.N." (see Abbreviations).

25. [Request for Information], *Gent. Mag.*, new ser., CI (June 1831), 482.

    Here, FM asks for information that might lead to the recovery of the original will of Queen Mary I, once in the possession of Mr. Hale of Alderly in Gloucestershire, but subsequently lost (see Bib. No. 26).

26. *Privy Purse Expenses of the Princess Mary, Daughter of*
     King Henry the Eighth, Afterwards Queen Mary ..., by
     Frederick Madden, Esq., F.S.A., Assistant Keeper of the
     MSS. in the British Museum, London: William Pickering,
     1831.

     Begun in September 1828 immediately after the publica-
     tion of *Havelok* and perhaps initially inspired by such
     works as that of Nicolas (see Bib. No. 22), the *Privy*
     Purse Expenses is among the most attractive of FM's
     works to the general reader. As he shows, these rec-
     ords, covering the period 1536 to 1544, provide close
     information about the "history, genealogy, and biography
     of the sovereigns, nobles, and gentry of England, whilst
     the most ample and curious illustrations of ancient man-
     ners and customs are held out to the lover of our na-
     tional antiquities." FM dedicated his book to Francis
     Douce, an early nineteenth-century Keeper of Manuscripts
     in the Museum, but he seems privately to have intended
     it also as a compliment to his fiancée, Mary Hayton, for
     in the early stages of working on this project he noted
     in his Diary, "The Princess Mary (I do love that name!)."
     In his prefatory material, FM states that his source was
     a MS. in the Royal Collection, and he also includes a
     full "memoir" of the Princess Mary, writing admittedly
     to correct the monstrous stereotype of Queen Mary Tudor
     that had grown up. The book includes an elaborate set
     of appendices providing inventories of jewels and por-
     traits and also the Queen's will, taken from a copy,
     since the original was not recovered (see Bib. No. 25).
     The completed work was delivered to FM 16 Sept. 1831.
     D, 30 Sept.; 19 Oct. 1828; 2 July, 17 Oct. 1829; 19
     Aug., 4 Dec. 1830; 5 Jan., 3 Mar., 30 July, 25 Aug., 16
     Sept. 1831; 28 Jan. 1832.

27. [Naval Costume temp. Elizabeth through James I], *Gent.*
     Mag., new ser., CI (Oct. 1831), 293.

     Signed "Nauticus" (see Abbreviations).

28. [On the Family of Gunning], *Gent. Mag.*, new ser., CI
     (Dec. 1831), 584-86.

     Signed "F.M."

29. [Extracts from an Account of the Library of John Aymon],
     Gent. Mag., new ser., CII (Jan. 1832), 30-32.

     Signed "C.N." (see Abbreviations).

30. "Historical Remarks on the Introduction of the Game of
    Chess into Europe, and on Ancient Chessmen Discovered in
    the Isle of Lewis," *Arch.*, XXIV (1831-32), 203-91.

    "By Frederic Madden, Esq., F.R.S., in a Letter to Henry
    Ellis, Esq., F.R.S., Secretary." Read 16 Feb. and 15
    Mar. 1832. Several references to this paper appear in
    Gent. Mag., new ser., CI (Dec. 1831), 551; CII (Feb.
    1832), 160; (Mar. 1832), 255; and (May 1832), 445-51,
    the last consisting of an abstract of the contribution.
    D, 15 Mar. 1832.

31. "Fragment of an Ancient Law Treatise" [MS. Cotton Domi-
    tian A. VIII.] in C[harles] P[urton] Cooper, *An Account
    of the most important Public Records of Great Britain
    and the Publications of the Record Commissioners* ...,
    2 vols. (London: Baldwin and Cradock, 1832), II, 412-24.

    Cooper, a barrister and secretary to the Record Commis-
    sion, was zealous in the recovery and publication of old
    legal documents. In January 1832, he called on FM for
    assistance in the transcription of the preface to a Lat-
    in translation of Old English laws codified under Edward
    the Confessor. In referring to this task in his Diary,
    FM sometimes alludes to the codifier as Ulpianus de Ed-
    wardo, evidently comparing him with the important third-
    century Roman jurist and imperial official, Domitian Ul-
    pianus. FM was paid eight gns. for his work, but no
    credit was given him in the published book. D, 7 Jan.,
    19 Mar., 23 May, etc. 1832.

32. *The Ancient English Romance of William and the Werwolf*,
    edited from an unique copy in King's College Library
    Cambridge, by Frederic Madden, Esq., F.R.S., F.S.A.,
    M.R.I.A., Assistant Keeper of MSS. in the British Museum.
    The Roxburghe Club, London: William Nicol, Shakspeare
    Press, 1832.

    As FM notes in his introduction, this romance first came
    to light in 1781, when Jacob Bryant published a defense
    of the authenticity of Chatterton's poems and included
    citations from the hitherto unnoticed *William and the
    Werwolf* in MS. King's College, Cambridge, 13. In his
    Ancient Metrical Tales (1829), C.H. Hartshorne printed
    the first several hundred lines of the same romance.
    FM's interest was first aroused when, in September 1830,
    Thomas Dibdin, librarian to Lord Spencer and an eccen-
    tric bibliophile, urged him to undertake an edition of
    the entire poem under the auspices of John Frederick

Campbell, Earl of Cawdor. In his Diary, FM observes
that he has no objection to carrying out the assignment
provided, "like Southey, it is made worth my while."
During the following year, he was able to transcribe the
MS. and compile the glossary, but he was then obliged,
rather against his better judgment, to include in the
work two letters on werewolves by the Hon. A. Herbert,
which Lord Cawdor brought to him. In May 1832, FM's
three copies of the finished work were delivered to him
together with Lord Cawdor's draft for one hundred pounds.
The 5540 alliterative lines of the romance, it may be
noted, were set in black letter. In 1867, W.W. Skeat,
in writing FM about a reedition of this work, which he
called *William of Palerne*, stated that the 1832 edition
left nothing to be desired and that he, Skeat, would be
serving merely as a printer's reader. D, 3-4 Sept.
1830; 16 Jan., 17, 27 Feb., 16 Nov., 13, 17, 26-31 Dec.
1831; 11, 26 May 1832.

33. [Inquiry about Ancient Chessmen], *Gent. Mag.*, new ser.,
     CII (May 1832), 391-92.

     Signed "F. Madden."

34. [Letters from Mr. Pinkerton to Bishop Percy], *Gent.
     Mag.*, new ser., CII (Aug. 1832), 121-25.

     Signed "F.M."

35. "Letters of Dr. Thomas Campbell to the Bishop of Dro-
     more," *Gent. Mag.*, new ser., CII (Nov. 1832), 409-13.

     Signed "F.M."

36. [Comment on a Mistaken Reading of a Gravestone Inscrip-
     tion in Lyson's History of Cumberland], *Gent. Mag.*, new
     ser., CIII (May 1833), 408-09.

     Signed "M." (see Abbreviations).

37. [Remarks on the Glossary to Sir Walter Scott's *Sir Tris-
     trem*], *Gent. Mag.*, new ser., CIII (Oct. 1833), 307-12.

     Signed "F.M." D, 8 Sept. 1833.

38. *Illuminated Ornaments, Selected from Manuscripts and
     Early Printed Books from the Sixth to the Seventeenth
     Centuries*, Drawn and Engraved by Henry Shaw, F.S.A.,
     with Descriptions by Sir Frederic Madden, K.H., F.R.S.,

F.S.A., M.R.S.L., Hon. M.R.I.A., Corr. F.S.A.E., Assistant Keeper of the MSS. in the British Museum, London:
William Pickering, 1833.

Introduction, pp. 1-16, signed "F.M." The work contains
fifty-nine beautifully colored plates, each with a description by FM. D, 14 Aug., 1 Nov. 1833; 17 Mar. 1845.

39. "Account of the Sale of Bishops' Lands, Between the
     Years 1637 and 1651," *CTG*, I (1834), 1-8, 122-27, 284-
     92.

     The authorship of this three-part paper is not indicated,
     but reference is made to it in the partial list of FM's
     publications included in the obituary notice by the Roy-
     al Society of Literature (see Bib. No. 286).

40. "Extracts from the Chronicle or Cartulary of the Abbey
     of Meaux, Co. York, Containing the Genealogies of Scur-
     res, Hyldeyhard, and Stutevyll," *CTG*, I (1834), 9-13.

     Signed "M."

41. "On the Knowledge Possessed by Europeans of the Elephant
     in the Thirteenth Century," *The Graphic and Historical
     Illustrator*, ed. Edward W. Brayley (London: C. Whitting-
     ham, 1834), 335-36, 352.

     Signed "F.M." A brief note about the first elephant
     known to have been sent to England, a gift of the King
     of France in 1255. Matthew Paris's history (Bib. No.
     148) provides the authority for this event, and a pic-
     ture of the elephant occurring in a manuscript copy of
     Matthew's chronicle is reproduced here, p. 352. That
     the signature "F.M." identifies the author as Madden,
     despite FM's reticence on the subject in his Diary and
     correspondence, is placed beyond doubt by a reference to
     him in the editor's preface. Brayley also explains that
     the essays in his collection were originally intended
     for a projected periodical, *The Graphic and Historical
     Illustrator*, which, owing to the publisher's failure, was
     abandoned. FM's lifelong fascination with exotic ani-
     mals, especially the elephant and hippopotamus, in the
     zoological gardens, is mentioned in the biographical
     sketch (Part One). We are indebted to Prof. A.S.G. Ed-
     wards for calling this publication to our attention.

42. "Abbats of Tichfield Abbey, in Hampshire," *CTG*, I (1834),
     14-16.

     Signed "F.M."

43. "Syon Monastery, Middlesex," *CTG*, I (1834), 29-32.
     Signed "F.M."

44. "Derbyshire Church Notes," *CTG*, I (1834), 34-51.
     Signed "M."

45. "List of Monastic Cartularies at Present Existing or
     Known to have existed since the Dissolution of Religious
     Houses," *CTG*, I (1834), 73-79, 197-208, 399-403; II
     (1835), 102-14.
     Each of the four parts signed "P. & M." (See Abbrevia-
     tions).

46. "Bateman Correspondence," *Gent. Mag.*, new ser., I (May
     1834), 478-84.
     Signed "M."

47. "Genealogical and Historical Notes from Ancient Calen-
     dars, ...," *CTG*, I (1834), 277-83, 395-98; II (1835),
     174-78, 376-78.
     Signed "M." A continuation in the same periodical but
     by another writer signing himself "J.G.N." appears in
     CTG, VI (1840), 90-98.

48. "On the Progress of Anglo-Saxon Literature in England,"
     Gent. Mag., new ser., II (Nov. 1834), 483-86.

     Signed "K.N." (see Abbreviations). Here, FM acknowl-
     edges that Kemble's strictures about the ignorance of
     Old English on the part of editors of old texts are jus-
     tified. He further points out errors in Sharon Turner's
     History of England during the Middle Ages. D, 20 Oct.
     1834.

49. [Remarks about some Semi-Saxon Words in Thorpe's Glos-
     sary to his *Analecta*], *Gent. Mag.*, new ser., II (Dec.
     1834), 591-94.
     Signed "K.N."

50. "Abstracts of Inquisitions Post Mortem, temp. Hen. III,
     for the Counties of Somerset and Dorset," *CTG*, II (1835),
     48-56, 168-74.
     Signed "M."

51. "The Parisian Omnibus of the Seventeenth Century," *Gent. Mag.*, new ser., III (May 1835), 475-80.

    Signed "F.M."

52. "Narratives of the Arrival of Louis de Bruges, Seigneur de la Gruthuyse, in England and of his Creation as Earl of Winchester, in 1472," *Arch.*, XXVI (1835-36), 265-86.

    "Communicated in a Letter from Sir Frederic Madden, K.H., F.R.S., etc., to Hudson Gurney, Esq., Vice Pres." Read 12 June 1835.

53. "Burning of the Queen's Store-Houses at Portsmouth in 1557," *CTG*, II (1835), 251-52.

    Signed "M."

54. "Burials at Chacombe Priory, Co. Northampton," *CTG*, II (1835), 388-89.

    Signed "M."

55. "Extracts from the Annals of Crokesden Abbey, Co. Stafford," *CTG*, II (1835), 297-310.

    Signed "F.M."

56. "Warrant of King James the First to the Great Wardrobe for Apparel, etc., for the Marriage of the Princess Elizabeth," *Arch.*, XXVI (1835-36), 380-94.

    "Communicated by Sir Frederic Madden, K.H., F.R.S., and S.A., in a Letter to Sir Henry Ellis, K.H., F.R.S., Secretary." Read 19 Nov. 1835.

57. "Remembrances for the Apparel, Accoutrements, and Necessaries of Henry Algernon Percy, Earl of Northumberland, in 1513," *Arch.*, XXVI (1835-36), 395-405.

    "By Sir Frederic Madden, K.H., F.R.S., and S.A., in a Letter to Charles George Young, Esq., York Herald." Read 24 Dec. 1835.

58. "Leland's Unpublished Notes of Staffordshire Families, and an Unpublished Fragment of his Itinerary," *CTG*, III (1836), 338-44.

    Signed "M."

59. "Expenses of Ancient Funeral Hearses at Westminster Ab-
     bey," *CTG*, III (1836), 380-81.

     Signed "M."

60. "Alchuine's Bible in the British Museum," *Gent. Mag.*,
     new ser., VI (Oct., Nov., and Dec. 1836), 358-63, 468-
     77, 580-87.

     Signed "F.M." For a discussion of the position FM takes
     in this paper, see Munby, *Connoisseurs* (Bib. No. 289).

61. "Observations on an Autograph of Shakspere, and the Or-
     thography of his Name," *Arch.*, XXVII (1836-37), 113-23.

     "In a Letter from Sir Frederic Madden, K.H., F.R.S.,
     and S.A., to John Gage, Esq., F.R.S., Director." Read
     26 Jan. 1837. Rpr. in 1838 (see Bib. No. 67). FM's
     conclusions in this matter aroused no little controver-
     sy. For example, some eight letters supporting or de-
     nouncing his position appeared in *Gent. Mag.* D, 21, 26
     Jan., 13 Apr. 1837; 7 Apr. 1838.

62. "Documents Relating to Perkin Warbeck, with Remarks on
     his History," *Arch.*, XXVII (1836-37), 153-210.

     "Letter to the Rt. Honourable the Earl of Aberdeen,
     Pres., S.A., from Sir Frederic Madden, K.H., F.R.S.,
     F.S.A." Read 6, 13, and 20 Apr. 1837. D, 6 Apr. 1837.

63. "Remarks on the Matrix of the Seal of Boxgrave Priory,
     in Sussex," *Arch.*, XXVII (1836-37), 375-80.

     "Sir Frederic Madden, K.H., F.R.S., F.S.A., in a Letter
     to Sir Henry Ellis, K.H., F.R.S., Secretary S.A." Read
     9 Mar. 1837. See also Bib. No. 144.

64. "Pedigree of the Frecheville and Musard Families, Lords
     of Crich and Staveley, in Derbyshire, ... with Numerous
     Additions and Corrections by Sir F. Madden," *CTG*, IV
     (1837), 1-28, 181-218.

     Signed "Sir F. Madden." Note also "Additions to the
     Pedigree of the Freschville [sic] Family, and a Few Cor-
     rections," by Joseph Hunter, *CTG*, IV (1837), 384-88.

65. "Saxon Charters to Thorney Abbey, in Cambridgeshire,"
     CTG, IV (1837), 54-59.

     Signed "M."

66. "Marriage Contract of Sir John Stafford and Anne Daughter of William Lord Botreaux, 1426," *CTG*, IV (1837), 249-55.

     Signed "F.M."

67. *Observations on an Autograph of Shakspere, and the Orthography of his Name*, London: Thomas Rodd, 1838. Rpr. from *Arch.*, XXVII (1836-37), 113-23.

     This pamphlet reproduces the original paper (Bib. No. 61) but also includes an additional note by FM dated 11 Apr. 1838. D, 11, 12, 13 Apr., 1 May 1838.

68. *The Old English Versions of the Gesta Romanorum: Edited for the First Time from Manuscripts in the British Museum and University Libraries, Cambridge*, by Sir Frederic Madden, K.H., F.R.S., M.R.I.A., Corr. F.S.A.E., Keeper of the MSS. in the British Museum, Roxburghe Club, London: W. Nicol, Shakspeare Press, 1838.

     As indicated in the biographical sketch in Part One, FM profited greatly from the Rev. J.J. Conybeare's hospitality in his splendid private library. There he first saw, and took extracts from, a fifteenth-century MS. containing the *Gesta Romanorum*, a work he had read about in Warton's *History of English Poetry*. Long afterwards, FM expanded his original entry on this experience in his 1824 Diary with the information that the MS. he had copied in Batheaston was given to the British Museum by the Rev. William Conybeare, who had inherited it from his brother. The desirability of editing the English *Gesta*, then available only in early printed books, occurred to FM at least by 1826, but not until 1837 was he able to launch the project in earnest. In June of that year, the Roxburghe Club approved his plans for the work, and he then proceeded with the transcription and collation of the several MSS. and researches into the background of the many tales. While on his wedding trip in September 1837, he took time to examine MSS. containing the Latin *Gesta* at Winchester Cathedral. And when in Paris in mid-1838, he looked over an illustrated printed copy in the Bibliothèque de l'Arsenal. Finally, in December 1838, he received his copies of the book from the printers. D, 2 Jan., 4, 14 Feb. 1824; 10 Nov. 1832; 26 Dec. 1834; 21 June, 21 Sept. 1837; 15 Jan., 3 Feb., 13 May, 9-10 June, 14 Aug., 17 Oct., 13 Dec. 1838.

69. *How the Goode Wif Thaught hir Doughter*, London: C. Whit-
     tingham, 1838. Short preface by FM.

     FM first came upon this short poem (175 lines) in 1831
     when, along with Forshall, he called on the Rev. Dr.
     Adam Clarke. Clarke showed them not only his Wycliffe
     MS., the object of their visit, but also a fifteenth-
     century MS. containing *How the Goode Wif*. The MS. was
     later sold to C.W. Loscombe of Pickwick Hall who arrang-
     ed for the printing of the poem at his own expense. FM
     was asked to correct the text, which was set in black
     letter, and to write a preface. He took the further
     trouble to collate the Loscombe version with that in a
     Trinity College, Cambridge, MS. FM was given seven cop-
     ies of the fifty printed. D, 6 Aug. 1831; 7 Nov. 1837;
     26 Jan., 15, 19 Feb., 18 Apr., 21 May 1838; 15 Nov.
     1839.

70. *Syr Gawayne; A Collection of Ancient Romance-Poems, by
     Scotish and English Authors, Relating to that Celebrated
     Knight of the Round Table*, by Sir Frederic Madden, K.H.,
     Bannatyne Club Publications 61, London, 1839.

     The evolution of FM's notable collection of Middle Eng-
     lish Gawain poems has been discussed by Ackerman (Bib.
     No. 248), and many others have commented on his editing
     of the centerpiece of the collection, *Sir Gawain and the
     Green Knight*, in MS. Cotton Nero A. X. Upon learning
     that Richard Price, who had earlier taken notice of that
     romance, no longer intended to publish it himself, FM
     added this undertaking to his already overextended com-
     mitments. Two conversations with Sir Walter Scott in
     October 1831 led him to plan the incorporation in the
     book of two other "Scotch" poems dealing with Gawain.
     But, seemingly in consequence of his immersion in the
     chronicle tradition of Arthur, as he encountered it in
     his work on *Laȝamons Brut*, he broadened his conception
     still further. That is, he decided to include all the
     English Gawain romances and ballads known to him. With
     the last-minute addition of *The Wedding of Sir Gawen and
     Dame Ragnell*, the collection of eleven poems was pub-
     lished in October 1839, a monument of literary scholar-
     ship. D, 9 July 1829; 6, 17 Oct. 1831; 24 Apr. 1832; 5,
     25 Aug., 1 Sept., 29 Nov. 1836; 11 Feb., 3 May 1837; 1
     Oct., 12 Nov. 1838; 16 Jan., 27 July, 22 Oct., 2 Dec.
     1839.

71. "Abstract of a Fragment of a Cartulary of Hexham Abbey, Northumberland," *CTG*, VI (1840), 38-46.

    Signed "M. & N." (see Abbreviations).

72. Thomas Warton, *The History of English Poetry from the Close of the Eleventh Century to the Commencement of the Eighteenth Century*, from the Edition of 1824 superintended by the late Richard Price, ... now further improved by the Corrections and Additions of Several Eminent Antiquaries [ed. Richard Taylor], 3 vols., London: Thomas Tegg, 1840.

    Initially published in three volumes appearing *seriatim* in 1774, 1778, and 1781 (Bib. No. 316), Warton's famous history was expanded and emended by a series of editors in the nineteenth century. FM's thorough acquaintance with Richard Price's edition of 1824 (Bib. No. 317) stood him in good stead in his earliest scholarly efforts, and he was requested by the two succeeding editors, Richard Taylor and W. Carew Hazlitt (Bib. No. 154), to supply further material for their reissues of 1840 and 1871. Hazlitt testifies that the greatest single improvement represented by Taylor's edition was the body of notes contributed by FM. D, 7 Jan., 19-20 Dec. 1837; 1 Feb., 24 Apr., 15 June 1838; 20 Oct. 1840.

73. [Autograph Signature of Shakspere], *Gent. Mag.*, new ser., XIII (Mar. 1840), 262-64.

74. "Destruction of Valuable Exchequer Papers," *Times*, 10 Mar. 1840, p. 5.

    Signed "Scrutator" (see Abbreviations). D, 10 Mar. 1840.

75. [Shakspere in Deed of 1612-13], *Gent. Mag.*, new ser., XIV (July 1840), 35-37.

    Signed "F.M."

76. Hrotswitha, *Gallicanus*, synopsis in A. Bruce-Whyte, *Histoire des langues romanes et de leur littérature depuis leur origine jusqu'au XIVe siècle*, 3 vols. (Paris: Treuttel et Würtz, 1841), I, 394-408.

    In 1826, when FM was happy to perform any literary hackwork that would augment his income, he was engaged by a scholar he called Whyte to write out an analysis of the

Latin plays of Hrotswitha (fl. 985). This he did
promptly and was pleased to receive a ten-pound note in
payment. Fifteen years passed before his analysis of
the play *Gallicanus* saw print in a chapter of the survey of Romance literature by Whyte, now called Bruce-
Whyte. No acknowledgment of FM's work is given in the
book. D, 1, 7, 10 Jan. 1826.

77. *Chronica Jocelin de Brakelonda. De Rebus Gestis Sam-
     sonis Abbatis Monasterii Sancti Edmondi*, ed. John Gage
     Rokewode, Camden Society XIII, London, 1840.

     FM was somewhat aggrieved on finding that his friend
     Rokewode had not included in his work any recognition
     of the assistance he had rendered in the preparation of
     this edition. D, 27 Oct. 1840.

78. "Letter Containing Intelligence of the Proceedings of
     the Court and Nobility, at the Commencement of the Year
     1454," *Arch.*, XXIX (1841-42), 305-17.

     "Addressed by Sir Frederic Madden, K.H., F.R.S., F.S.A.,
     to John Gage Rokewode, Esq., Director, S.A." Read 24
     Feb. 1842.

79. "Political Poems of the Reigns of Henry VI. and Edward
     IV.," *Arch.*, XXIX (1841-42), 318-47.

     "Communicated by Sir Frederic Madden, K.H., in a Letter
     to John Gage Rokewode, Esq., Director, S.A." Read 10
     Mar. 1842.

80. "Warrant Signed by Edward Vth as King," *Arch.*, XXX
     (1843-44), 545.

     A document, "probably unique in regard to signatures,"
     was exhibited by FM, 24 Nov. 1842.

81. [Prayer Book of Sigismund I, King of Poland], *Gent.
     Mag.*, new ser., XXIII (July 1845), 25-28.

     Signed "M."

82. *Laʒamons Brut, or Chronicle of Britain; A Poetical Semi-
     Saxon Paraphrase of the Brut of Wace*, ..., Accompanied
     by a Literal Translation, Notes, and a Grammatical Glos-
     sary, by Sir Frederic Madden, K.H., Keeper of the MSS.
     in the British Museum, 3 vols., Society of Antiquaries
     of London, London, 1847.

FM's attention was first drawn to Layamon in 1824 when, while serving as copyist to Petrie, he had occasion to examine MS. Cotton Caligula A. IX. containing the earlier text of the *Brut*. Petrie suggested that he edit the work, only a few extracts of which had been printed at that time. In about 1827, while Josiah Forshall was Keeper of Manuscripts in the Museum, a portion of the supposedly destroyed MS. Cotton Otho C. XIII., providing a second and somewhat later text of Layamon, came to light. Subsequently, FM came on more damaged leaves belonging to that MS., and he soon began the task of editing the entire chronicle. The process of transcribing the two texts, running to some thirty thousand half-lines, the translation, the compiling of grammatical notes and glossary, and the reception of the work by the earliest reviewers have been briefly treated by Ackerman (Bib. No. 249). D, 17 Aug. 1824; 17 Feb. 1825; 14 Aug. 1826; 21 Aug. 1829; 11 Dec. 1830; 20 May, 15 Sept., 15 Dec. 1831; 27 Apr., 15 May 1832; 15 Apr., 19-20 Aug. 1833; 1 Feb. 1834; 23 Apr., 9 Oct., 22 Nov. 1835; 23 Apr. 1836; 18 Dec. 1837; 8, 15, 26 Jan. 1839; 31 Dec. 1842; 13 Mar., 5 Apr. 1843; 7, 27 Feb., 1 Mar. 1844; 19 May 1845; 2, 19, 30 Mar. 1847; 6 Mar., 3 Apr. 1848; 5, 18 Apr. 1854; 25 May 1871. For FM's personal copy with annotations, see Bib. No. 232.

83. "Sanuto's Doges of Venice," *N&Q*, I (No. 3, 17 Nov. 1849), 35-36.

Signed "Frederick Madden."

84. "MSS. of the Wycliffite Translations of the Scriptures," *N&Q*, I (No. 23, 6 Apr. 1850), 366.

Signed "F. Madden."

85. "Queries Respecting Purvey on the Apocalypse and Bonner on the Seven Sacraments," *N&Q*, I (No. 28, 11 May 1850), 452.

Signed "F. Madden."

86. J[oseph] B[althazar] Silvestre, *Universal Palaeography: or Fac-Similes of Writings of all Nations and Periods*, ..., Translated from the French and Edited with Corrections and Notes, by Sir Frederic Madden, K.H., F.R.S., M.R.I.A., 2 vols., London: Bohn, 1850.

Silvestre's reputable and useful *Paléographie univer-
selle*, illustrated with many plates, was originally published in four volumes, 1839 to 1841. In July 1847, FM
agreed to prepare a translation for the London publisher
Bohn. In order to speed the process, FM engaged a
translator, Westwood. In his Diary, FM speaks of his
painstaking revision of the work and of his annoyance
over Westwood's proprietary attitude toward it. Bohn
advertised the new work in April 1850, pricing the two
volumes of the text alone at one pound, sixteen shillings, and the edition with Silvestre's plates at far
more. D, 6 July 1847; 18 May 1848; 27 Aug. 1849; 20
Apr., 2 July 1850.

87.   *The Holy Bible, Containing the Old and New Testaments,
with the Apocryphal Books, in the Earliest English Versions, made from the Latin Vulgate by John Wycliffe and
his Followers,* ed. by the Rev. Josiah Forshall, F.R.S.,
etc., Late Fellow of Exeter College, and Sir Frederic
Madden, K.H., F.R.S., etc., Keeper of the MSS. in the
British Museum, 4 vols., Oxford: Oxford University
Press, 1850.

A critical edition of the Wycliffe Bible was first pro-
jected by the Rev. Henry Baber, Keeper of Printed Books
at the Museum. In 1829, however, Baber enlisted the aid
of Josiah Forshall and then that of FM as well. Shortly
thereafter, he himself withdrew from the task. Because
of the immense amount of collation and transcription
involved, the Bible came to be the most laborious of
all FM's undertakings, and the more so because Forshall's recurring bouts of mental illness threw a dis-
proportionate share of the burden on his shoulders. For
the New Testament alone, eighteen MSS. were collated for
the earlier version and thirty-nine for the later. The
writing of the preface was left largely to FM and the
glossary was also his responsibility. The completion
of the printing was commemorated in the name bestowed
on his youngest son, born in 1850, as indicated in the
life sketch. Each of the editors received an honorarium
of five hundred pounds and a copy of the work. Also in
1850, the preface and glossary were issued in separate
form. D, 31 May, 28, 30 Nov. 1829; 26 Mar. 1831; 7
Feb.-13 Mar. 1841; 29 July 1847; 20 July 1848; 7 May, 20
June, 12, 21 Oct., 16, 30 Nov., 4 Dec. 1850. *The Books
of Job, Psalms, Proverbs, Ecclesiastes, and the Song of
Solomon according to the Wycliffite Version made by
Nicholas de Hereford about A.D. 1381,* Oxford: Clarendon
Press, 1881. A rpr. of a portion of the above.

88. "Beatrix Lady Talbot," *N&Q*, III (No. 62, 4 Jan. 1851), 10.

    Signed "F. Madden."

89. "Charles the First and Bartolomeo Della Nave's Collection of Pictures," *N&Q*, III (No. 74, 29 Mar. 1851), 236.

    Signed "F. Madden."

90. "Poems of John Seguard of Norwich," *N&Q*, III (No. 75, 26 Apr. 1851), 261-62.

    Signed "F.M."

91. "The Duke of Monmouth's Pocket-Books," *N&Q*, IV (No. 88, 5 July 1851), 1-3.

    Signed "F. Madden." D, 5 July 1851.

92. "Anthony Mundy," *N&Q*, IV (No. 91, 26 July 1851), 55-56.

    Signed "F. Madden."

93. [Gold Ring Found at Sessa in the Kingdom of Naples], *AJ*, VIII (1851), 418-20.

    "Exhibited by Sir Frederic Madden by favour of George Borett, Esq., of Southampton before the Archaeological Institute."

94. "Perkin Warbeck," *N&Q*, IV (No. 107, 15 Nov. 1851), 377.

    Signed "F. Madden." D, 15 Nov. 1851.

95. "Longueville MSS.," *N&Q*, V (No. 114, 3 Jan. 1852), 17.

    Signed "F. Madden."

96. "St. George's Heraldical MSS.," *N&Q*, V (No. 124, 13 Mar. 1852), 253-54.

    Signed "μ." D, 13 Mar. 1852.

97. [Ancient Riddle in a Collection of Quaint Enigmas in a MS. of the 13th Century, MS. Cotton Cleopatra B. IX.], *AJ*, IX (1852), 97-98.

98. "The Trusty Servant at Winchester," *N&Q*, VI (No. 140, 3 July 1852), 12-13.

    Signed "F. Madden."

99.   "Portrait Painters of Queen Elizabeth," *N&Q*, VI (No.
       150, 11 Sept. 1852), 237-39.

       Signed "F. Madden."

100.   "Differences between Copies of the Folio Editions of
       Shakspere," *N&Q*, VI (No. 159, 13 Nov. 1852), 469-70.

       Signed "F. Madden."

101.   "Rufus's Oak and Stone," *N&Q*, VI (No. 164, 18 Dec.
       1852), 581-82.

       Signed "F. Madden."

102.   "Autograph of Edward of Lancaster, Son of Henry VI,"
       N&Q, VII (No. 167, 8 Jan. 1853), 33-34.

       Signed "F. Madden." D, 8 Jan. 1853.

103.   [Dunsby Font, Lincolnshire], *AJ*, X (1853), 173.

       FM points out the significance of letters carved on a
       panel of an old font at this location.

104.   "Was Thomas Lord Lyttleton the Author of Junius's Let-
       ters?" *N&Q*, VIII (No. 193, 9 July 1853), 31-33.

       Signed "F. Madden."

105.   "Bale MSS. Referred to in Tanner's 'Bibliotheca Bri-
       tannico-Hibernica,'" *N&Q*, VIII (No. 205, 1 Oct. 1853),
       311-12.

       Signed "F. Madden." For Tanner, see Bib. No. 241.

106.   "The 'Ancren Riwle,'" *N&Q*, IX (No. 219, 7 Jan. 1854),
       5-6.

       Signed "F. Madden." A review of James Morton's edition
       of this work. D, 29 Dec. 1853; 7 Jan. 1854.

107.   "Examples of Mediaeval Seals, Illustrations of the Mode
       of Sealing *En Placard*," *AJ*, XI (1854), 261-69.

       Signed "F. Madden." Seal and charter of Eudes, King
       of France, 888 or 889. D, 9 Oct. 1854.

108.   *A Relation of Some Abuses which are Committed against
       the Common-Wealth, together with a Freindlie Reprehen-
       sion of the Same. Composed especiallie for the Benefit*

of the Countie of Durham, December the xxvjth, 1629,
ed. Sir Frederic Madden, K.H., F.R.S., *Camden Miscel-
lany*, Vol. III, Camden Society LXI (1854).

A fifty-four-page tract. D, 13 Dec. 1854.

109. "Bishops' Arms," *N&Q*, XI (No. 278, 24 Feb. 1855), 145.
Signed "F. Madden."

110. "Phillips's 'New World of Words,'" *N&Q*, XI (No. 281,
17 Mar. 1855), 208-09.
Signed "F. Madden." Comments about Phillips's lexi-
cographical work. D, 14 Apr. 1855.

111. "Bishops' Arms," *N&Q*, XI (No. 281, 17 Mar. 1855), 214.
Signed "F.M."

112. "Agreement between the Dean and Chapter of St. Paul's,
London, and Walter, the Orgoner of Southwark, Relating
to a Clock, 22 Nov. 1344," *AJ*, XII (1855), 173-77.
"Communicated by Sir F. Madden, K.H."

113. "Copy of the 'Assertio Septem Sacramentorum adversus
Lutherum,' Presented by Henry VIII. to the Pope in
1521," *N&Q*, XII (No. 297, 7 July 1855), 1-2.
Signed "F. Madden."

114. "*Gesta Romanorum*," *N&Q*, XII (No. 306, 8 Sept. 1855),
187.
Signed "F. Madden."

115. "Nero's Game of Chariots," *N&Q*, XII (No. 318, 1 Dec.
1855), 425.
Signed "F. Madden."

116. "Manuscripts Relating to Essex," *N&Q*, XII (No. 319, 8
Dec. 1855), 454-55.
Signed "F. Madden." D, 23 Nov. 1855.

117. "Pompey's Playing Tables," *N&Q*, XII (No. 322, 29 Dec.
1855), 518.
Signed "F. Madden." Evidently a response to an inquiry
on this subject appearing in *N&Q*, XII (No. 318, 1 Dec.

1855), 428, signed "μ," a signature also used by FM.
See Bib. No. 96.

118.   "Prose Chronicles of England Called the Brute," *N&Q*,
        2nd. ser., I (No. 1, 5 Jan. 1856), 1-4.

        Signed "F. Madden."

119.   [Letter from FM to the Editors of the *Athenaeum* pro-
        testing their published implication that the British
        Museum had purchased forged MSS. from Simonides], *Ath.*,
        No. 1480 (8 Mar. 1856), 298-99.

        D, 2, 4 Mar. 1856.

120.   "Ancient Monastic Libraries," *N&Q*, 2nd ser., I (No.
        25, 21 June 1856), 485-88.

        Signed "F. Madden." D, 17, 21 June 1856.

121.   "Oderigi of Gubbio," *Literary Gazette*, No. 12 (17 May
        1856), 279.

        Signed "F. Madden." Correction of an item in a sales
        catalogue.

122.   "Remarks on the Anglo-Saxon Charters [by Offa and
        Eadgar] Granted to the Abbey of St. Denis, in France,
        and on the Seals attached to them," *AJ*, XIII (1856),
        355-71.

        Signed "F. Madden." D, 16 June 1856.

123.   "Forged Roman 'Waxen Tablets,'" *N&Q*, 2nd ser., II (No.
        27, 5 July 1856), 5.

        Signed "F. Madden." D, 22 June 1856.

124.   "Götz von Berlichingen with the Iron Hand," *N&Q*, 2nd
        ser., II (No. 41, 11 Oct. 1856), 281.

        Signed "F. Madden." D, 28 Sept. 1856.

125.   "Ormonde Possessions in England," *N&Q*, 2nd ser., III
        (No. 53, 3 Jan. 1857), 19.

        Signed "F. Madden."

126.   "Latin Poems of Johannes Opicius: Manuscripts at White-
        hall, temp. Car. I.," *N&Q*, 2nd ser., III (No. 54, 10
        Jan. 1857), 21.

        Signed "F. Madden." D, 10 Jan. 1857.

127. "Visit of the Duke of Wurtemburg-Mumpelgard to James I., in 1610," *Illustrated London News*, XXX (28 Feb. 1857), 192.

Signed "F. Madden." D, 27 Feb. 1857.

128. "Writing with the Foot," *N&Q*, 2nd ser., III (No. 66, 4 Apr. 1857), 271-72.

Signed "F. Madden."

129. *Photographic Facsimiles of the Remains of the Epistles of Clement of Rome*, made from the unique copy preserved in the Codex Alexandrinus, ed. William Cureton, British Museum, 1856.

Preface by FM. For an account of the photographing of eleven leaves of the famous Codex Alexandrinus, see the biographical sketch, Part One. D, 12, 23, 25, 27 Feb., 1, 27 Mar., 15, 19, 21 Apr., 12, 20, 22 Oct. 1856.

130. "Richard Beauchamp, Earl of Warwick, as a Noble Author," *N&Q*, 2nd ser., V (No. 106, 9 Jan. 1858), 21-22.

Signed "F. Madden."

131. "Cost or Nedescost," *N&Q*, 2nd ser., V (No. 121, 24 Apr. 1858), 337-38.

Signed "μ." D, 5 Apr. 1858.

132. "The *Historia Britonum* of Geoffrey of Monmouth," *AJ*, XV (1858), 299-312.

Signed "F. Madden." D, 31 Dec. 1857; 1 Jan., 9 Oct. 1858.

133. "Gwillim's 'Heraldry,'" *N&Q*, 2nd ser., VI (No. 131, 3 July 1858), 10-11.

Signed "F. Madden."

134. "Ancient Painting at Cowdry," *N&Q*, 2nd ser., VI (No. 131, 3 July 1858), 17.

Signed "F. Madden."

135. [MS. Bought by Douce and Bequeathed to the British Museum], *N&Q*, 2nd ser., VI (No. 132, 10 July 1858), 38.

Signed "F. Madden."

136.   "Robert Nelson's Letters and Papers," *N&Q*, 2nd ser.,
        VI (No. 145, 9 Oct. 1858), 295.

        Signed "F. Madden."

137.   "Transcript of Matthew Paris Used by Archbishop Park-
        er," *N&Q*, 2nd ser., VI (No. 155, 18 Dec. 1858), 497.

138.   "Milton's Autograph in the Album of Christopher Ar-
        nold," *N&Q*, 2nd ser., VII (No. 157, 1 Jan. 1859), 3-4.

        Signed "F. Madden."

139.   "The Paston Letters," *N&Q*, 2nd ser., VII (No. 162, 5
        Feb. 1859), 108-09.

        Signed "F. Madden." D, 28 Jan., 5 Feb. 1859.

140.   "Cromwelliana," *N&Q*, 2nd ser., VII (No. 164, 19 Feb.
        1859), 141.

        Signed "F. Madden." D, 19 Feb. 1859.

141.   "Mr. Collier and the British Museum," *The Critic*, XX
        (No. 504, 3 Mar. 1860), 152.

        Letter defending the BM against Collier's attacks. D,
        21 Mar. 1860.

142.   "Mr. Collier and the British Museum," *Times*, 22 Mar.
        1860, p. 10.

        Signed "F. Madden." D, 21 Mar. 1860.

143.   "The Shakspeare Controversy," *N&Q*, 2nd ser., IX (No.
        222, 31 Mar. 1860), 255.

        FM protests the tone of some of the rejoinders to his
        proposal for the spelling of the name.

144.   [Inscription on the Edges of Seals, such as that of
        Boxgrave Priory], *AJ*, XVIII (1861), 71.

        Here FM alludes to his earlier paper on Boxgrave Priory
        (Bib. No. 63).

145.   [Matthew of Westminster Pertaining to an Inscription
        on the Edge of a Seal], *AJ*, XVIII (1861), 79.

146.   [On a Forged Charter of Edward the Confessor in the
        possession of the Earl of Winchelsea], *AJ*, XIX (1862),
        176.

This communication is referred to as one "of unusual interest" by the editor of *AJ*.

147. [Epitaph to Mouton], *N&Q*, 3rd ser., V (No. 128, 11 June 1864), 475.

Signed "M.M." (see Abbreviations). A four-line poem beginning "Ci repose pauvre Mouton." D, 11 June 1864.

148. *Matthaei Parisiensis Monachi Sancti Albani Historia Anglorum, sive vulgo dicitur Historia Minor*, ed. Sir Frederic Madden, K.H., Rolls Series 44, 3 vols., London, 1866-69.

As noted in the biographical sketch (Part One), the editing of the *Historia Minor*, covering the period 1067 to 1253, proved to be an onerous burden for FM. In June 1860, he confesses to a sense of regret at having accepted the assignment, and not until 1869, eleven years after beginning his task, was he able to turn in the corrected proofs of the third and final volume. FM's preface in Vol. I sets forth his opinion that much of the *Flores Historiarum*, said to be the work of the pseudo Matthew of Westminster, is in the handwriting of Matthew of Paris, a circumstance suggesting the latter's authorship. In 1871, however, he observes in his Diary that Hardy "negatives" such a conclusion. But see Vaughan's appraisal of FM's views (Bib. No. 314). D, 28 Apr., 6 May, 5 July, 13 Aug. 1858; 2 Aug., 3 Dec. 1859; 1 June, 23 Sept., 29 Nov., 11 Dec. 1860; 3 Mar., 6 Aug., 19 Dec. 1862; 7, 12, 23 Oct., 12 Nov. 1864; 9 Jan., 29 Apr., 30 Sept., 21 Nov. 1865; 18 Jan., 19 Feb., 22, 24 Sept., 31 Oct. 1866; 7 Jan., 29 May, 29 July 1867; 14 Jan., 9 Apr., 7 Oct. 1868; 15 Jan., 20, 23 Feb., 22 Apr. 1869; 25 Mar. 1871.

149. "Hogarth and Chatterton," *Times*, 25 May 1867, p. 5.

Signed "F. Madden." A brief letter pointing out the error of labeling a portrait of Chatterton in the South Kensington Museum as the work of Hogarth. D, 25 May 1867.

150. "Letters I. to VIII. Henry VII.," *Arch.*, XLI (1867), 69-71.

In May 1866, the Society of Antiquaries appointed a committee, including FM, which undertook a collation of the extant copies of the Paston letters [*Arch.*, XLI (1867), 38-53]. FM's report of his collation of the

letters assigned to him appears in the later issue of
Arch. designated above.

151.   "Sir Edward Coke's 'Household Book,' for 1596-7," *N&Q*,
       4th ser., I (No. 7, 15 Feb. 1868), 158.

       Signed "F. Madden."

152.   "The Charlemagne Bible," *Ath.*, No. 2196 (27 Nov. 1869),
       701.

       Signed "F. Madden." FM refers here to his three-part
       article on Alchuine's Bible written many years earlier
       (Bib. No. 60).

153.   "Garrison Chapel (or Church), Portsmouth," *N&Q*, 4th
       ser., V (No. 120, 16 Apr. 1870), 383.

       Signed "F.R.S." (see Abbreviations). D, 28 Oct. 1869;
       16 Apr. 1870.

154.   Thomas Warton, *The History of English Poetry*, ..., ed.
       W. Carew Hazlitt, 4 vols., London: Reeves and Turner,
       1871.

       See the biographical sketch, Part One, and Bib. Nos.
       72, 316, and 317. D, 1 Jan., 30 June 1868; 1 Jan., 27
       Dec. 1869; 18 May 1871.

SUPPLEMENT TO BIBLIOGRAPHY A

Representative Catalogues by Madden
or Prepared under his Supervision

[Mr. M.A.F. Borrie of the British Library has very kindly
pointed out to us that, as Keeper, FM was responsible for all
official publications issued by his department. Prominent
among such routine publications were lists of new acquisi-
tions, a task not seldom in arrears in periods of rapid ex-
pansion. Esdaile's *The British Museum Library* (Bib. No. 268)
provides information about catalogues produced by FM's department, and in T.C. Skeat's *The Catalogues of the Manuscript Collections of the British Museum* (Bib. No. 305), the
catalogues "in regular use" are given together with historical notes. Below are listed several works of this sort
which serve to illustrate the range of FM's professional con-
cerns. Included are two manuscript catalogues of earlier
date which are especially valuable because the copies kept in
the Students' Room of the Department of Manuscripts bear FM's
handwritten emendations and expansions.]

155. Samuel Ayscough, *A Catalogue of the Manuscripts Pre-
     served in the British Museum, Hitherto undescribed*, 2
     vols., London: John Rivington, 1782.

     As noted by T.C. Skeat (Bib. No. 305), FM rendered this
     work far more useful by cutting up, rearranging, and
     correcting a copy for use in his department. D, 7 Feb.
     1857, etc. This rearranged and corrected copy is on
     the open shelves of the Students' Room.

156. Joseph Planta, *A Catalogue of the Manuscripts of the
     Cottonian Library, Deposited in the British Museum*,
     Printed at the Command of his Majesty, King George III,
     1802.

     As indicated in the biographical sketch in Part One,
     FM recorded his numerous corrections and additions in

the margins of a copy of Planta's work while in the
process of restoring the Cotton Collection. This copy,
not normally available to the public, is kept in the
reference library of the Department of Manuscripts.

157. *Catalogue of the Manuscript Music in the British Museum*, by T. Oliphant and Sir Frederic Madden. Printed
by Order of the Trustees, 1842.

158. *Catalogue of the Maps, Charts, and Plans, and of the
Topographical Drawings in the British Museum*, ed. under
Sir Frederic Madden's supervision by the senior assistant in the Department of Manuscripts [John Holmes], 3
vols., Printed by Order of the Trustees, 1844, 1861,
rpr. 1962.

Circumstances connected with the preparation and is-
suance of this catalogue illustrate the enmity that
existed between FM and Panizzi, as Mr. Borrie has
called to our attention. After Holmes's death in 1853,
FM drew up a list of badly needed corrections and additions that, together with a fresh preface he had written, would appear as Vol. III of the catalogue. But
Panizzi, evidently in the interests of protecting
Holmes's reputation, suppressed the volume and not until 1962 was it published from sheets surviving from a
fire in the Museum bindery.

159. *A List of Autograph Letters, Original Charters, Great
Seals, and Manuscripts exhibited in the Department of
Manuscripts*, ed. Sir Frederic Madden, Printed by Order
of the Trustees, 1851. A new edition in 1859 is entitled *A Guide to the Autograph Letters, Manuscripts,
Original Charters, Baronial and Ecclesiastical Seals
...*, and later editions appeared in 1862 and 1866.

BIBLIOGRAPHY B

Autograph Material and Special Collections

Nearly all the important manuscripts, working papers, annotated books, and special collections are deposited in the
Department of Manuscripts of the British Library (BL), the
Department of Western Manuscripts of the Bodleian Library
(Bod.), Cambridge University Library (Camb.), the Houghton
Library, Harvard University (Harv.), and the Beinecke Library, Yale University (Yale). Shelf marks are supplied except for those materials classified as printed books. To
the annotated books listed here should be added three works
already cited in other sections of this bibliography (Nos.
4, 155, and 156).
     The items listed here are set forth under three head-
ings: I. Life Records, including Correspondence; II. Working
Papers, including Annotated books; and III. Special Collections and Miscellanea.

I. Life Records, including Correspondence

160. Diary of Sir Frederic Madden, 1819-73, 43 vols., Bod.
      MSS. Engl hist. c. 140-82.

      Munby (Bib. No. 289) has called this journal "the most
      fascinating unpublished book I know."

161. Private Memoirs, forming a supplement to "Mentis meae
      ratio in amore." Signed "F.M., Portsmouth, 1821." BL
      Add. MS. 57341.

162. Probate copy of FM's will, 1873. BL Add. Charter
      75755.

163. Legacy receipts and household inventory, 1873, with
      other papers. BL Add. MS. 57342.

The household inventory consists of an interesting list
of the furnishings, room by room, of the Maddens' rent-
ed house in St. Stephen's Square. Also included is
"A Sketch of the Life and Manners of Emily Mary (1)
Tedlie, (2) Holley, née Madden" by Frederic W. Madden,
FM's eldest son. An unflattering impression of Emily
Mary is given here. A draft letter by FM, likewise
included, marked "not sent," and dated 17 July 1834,
solicits matrimonial advice from "Mrs. Powell," an
aunt.

164. *Catalogue of the Important and Valuable Collection of
      Printed Books and Manuscripts Formed by the late Sir
      Frederic Madden, K.H., F.R.S., F.S.A., etc.*, to be sold
      at auction by Messrs. Sotheby, Wilkinson, and Hodge,
      Thursday, 7 August 1873 and two following days, London:
      Dryden Press, 1873.

      This twenty-five-page catalogue lists 1219 items, one
      of them being FM's collection of 27,500 ballads and
      songs, bound in twenty-five volumes (see Bib. No. 243).

165. Diaries and Memoranda of Sir Henry Ellis, 1813-49. BL
      Add. MS. 36653.

166. Selected Correspondence of Frederic Madden, 1823-70,
      12 vols. BL Egerton MSS. 2837-48.

      A mass of valuable letters including drafts of some of
      FM's replies. The correspondents include Thomas Car-
      lyle, the Earl of Cawdor, Frederick Furnivall, Lady
      Charlotte Guest, Henry Hallam, James Halliwell-Phillipps,
      John M. Kemble, Sir Edwin Landseer, Count Libri, Thomas
      Macaulay, William Morris, Sir Francis Palgrave, Coven-
      try Patmore, Sir Thomas Phillipps, Henry Crabb Robin-
      son, John Ruskin, The Duke of Rutland, Sir Walter Scott,
      Sydney Smirke, Earl Spencer, Benjamin Thorpe, and
      Thomas Wright. FM's ticket of admission to the reading
      room of the BM, dated 8 Dec. 1823, is pasted in Vol. I.

167. Letter by FM to Philip Bliss, 1825. Bod. MS. Eng.
      misc. d 91, fols. 186-92.

168. Correspondence of Philip Bliss. BL Add. MSS. 34567-
      34582.

      Many letters from FM are included.

169. Notes by Francis Douce of Douce's letters to FM, c. 1831. Bod. MS. Douce f. 11.

170. Letters to Francis Douce, 1829-32. Bod. MSS. Douce d. 26, fol. 188; d. 27, fol. 58; d. 28, fols. 22, 27; d. 30, fols. 158-70.

171. Letter of FM, 1836. Bod. MS. Eng. misc. d. 36, fols. 214-15.

172. Correspondence with Sir Thomas Phillipps, 1828-67. Bod. MSS. Phillipps-Robinson, *passim.*

173. Letters to T.M. Stone, 1839-41. Bod. MS. Eng. lett. d. 170, fols. 106-08.

174. Letters to J.B. Nichols, 1848. Bod. 13. Θ 96, p. viii.

    Letters inserted in a printed book.

175. Letters, various, 1856-58. Bod. MS. Eng. lett. d. 75, fols. 28, 139.

176. Letter of FM to T.J. Pettigrew and letter of Francis Douce to FM. Bod. MS. Douce d. 17, fols. 52, 69 (*S.C.*, 33373).

177. Letters addressed to John Gough Nichols as editor of *Gent. Mag.* Bod. MSS. Autogr. c. 1, fols. 334-35 (*S.C.*, 30420); Eng. misc. d. 37, fols. 177-86 (*S.C.*, 33396).

178. Letters of FM to J.G. Nichols, 1820-40. BL Add. MS. 5120A.

179. Autograph letters almost entirely of English librarians. Bod. MS. Autogr. d. 2 (*S.C.*, 31344).

    Letter of FM, fols. 63-64.

180. Letters concerning FM's work on the catalogue of the Holkham MSS. Bod. MS. Eng. misc. d. 99.

    See Bib. No. 230.

181. Correspondence of Sir Anthony Panizzi, 1840-66. BL Add. MSS. 36714-36729.

    Letter of FM, 1856. MS. 36717, fol. 457.

182. Letters with drafts of replies and papers relating to
     the Simonides, Payne Collier, and Hillier affairs.
     Bod. MS. Eng. misc. c. 96.

183. Letter of FM's executors to the Bodleian Library per-
     taining to the bequest of FM's Diary and other papers.
     Bod. MS. Add. A. 292, fols. 41–42 (*S.C.*, 29407).

184. Letter of FM. Camb. MS. Oo. 6. 89.

185. Letter to FM. Camb. MS. Add. 2688, fol. 62.

186. Letter of FM to Henry Austen, 10 May 1842. Harv. Auto-
     graph File.

187. Letter of FM to Richard Harris Barham, 20 Feb. 18??
     Harv. MS. Eng. 936 (I, 87).

188. Letter of FM to Jacob Henry Burn, 25 June 1846. Harv.
     fMS. Eng. 1178 (3. 96).

189. Two letters of FM to Francis James Child, 16 Nov. 1855,
     7 Jan. 1861. Harv. bMS. Am 1922 (185–86).

     These letters refer to queries about a new edition of
     the works of Chaucer. For Child's letters to FM, see
     Bib. No. 166. D, 26 Jan. 1856; 2 Jan. 1861.

190. Letter of FM to John Gorham Palfrey, 1856. Harv. bMS.
     Am 1704 (593).

[Scattered letters to and from FM pertaining to specialized
subjects are to be found in some collections of Working Papers (see especially Bib. No. 239).]

II. Working Papers, including Annotated Books

191. Proofs and revises of the introduction and notes for
     the editions of *Syr Gawayne* and *William and the Wer-
     wolf* (Bib. Nos. 70 and 32). BL, printed books.

192. Notes for the edition of Matthew Paris, *Historia Minor*
     (Bib. No. 148). BL Add. MS. 58080. (See Bib. Nos.
     205, 229.)

193. Notes for a history of the BM. BL Add. MS. 39971 (See
     Bib. No. 245.)

194. Autograph notes on the ballads in the Pepys collection.
     BL Add. MS. 33813, fol. 115.

195. C.H. Hartshorne, ed., *Ancient Metrical Tales, edited
     chiefly from Original Sources*, London: W. Pickering,
     1829. BL, printed books.

     This copy has marginalia representing FM's collation
     with MSS.

196. Joseph Ritson, ed., *Ancient Songs from the Time of King
     Kenry the Third to the Revolution*, London, printed for
     J. Johnson, 1790. BL Egerton MS. 3778.

     Annotated by FM. D, 15 Mar. 1825.

197. Sir Thomas Phillipps, *Catalogus librorum, manuscripto-
     rum, ...*, Middle Hill, 1837. BL Egerton MS. 2337.

     Marginal corrections by FM.

198. Notes on Early English MSS. BL Egerton MS. 2257.

199. *Radulphi, abbatis de Coggeshall, opera quae supersunt*,
     ed. John Dunkin, Neumagen, 1852. BL, printed books.

     Annotated by FM.

200. Notes on Venetian Ducali. BL Add. MS. 20758.

201. Translation of Old French *Lai d'Havelok* in FM's edition
     of *Havelok the Dane* (Bib. No. 7). BL, printed books.

202. Collections for FM's edition of *The Old English Ver-
     sions of the Gesta Romanorum* (Bib. No. 68). Bod. MS.
     Eng. misc. 76 (*S.C.*, 36096).

203. Collections for the grammatical analysis of FM's edi-
     tion of *Laʒamons Brut* (Bib. No. 82). Bod. MS. Eng.
     poet. c. 8 (*S.C.*, 32689).

204. Account of expenses incurred in the editing of Wy-
     cliffe's Bible (Bib. No. 87). Bod. MS. Eng. bib. c. 1
     (*S.C.*, 31011).

205. Transcription of Matthew Paris, *Historia Minor*, and
     other papers (Bib. No. 148). Bod. MS. Add. D. 86-88
     (*S.C.*, 29231-29233). (See Bib. Nos. 192, 229.)

206. Review by FM of works on hieroglyphics, with some let-
      ters, 1824. Bod. MS. Eng. misc. d. 100.

      One of FM's early projects. D, 11 Apr., 23, 28 Oct.,
      29 Nov. 1829, etc.

207. Memoranda relating to certain MSS. abstracted from
      Trinity College, Cambridge, and subsequently purchased
      for the BM out of Mr. J.O. Halliwell-Phillipps' collec-
      tion of MSS., 1866. Bod. MS. Eng. misc. f. 35.

208. Abstracts of trickings of seals. Bod. MS. Eng. misc.
      c. 128.

209. Autograph note. Camb. MS. Add. 1845.

210. Catalogue of Coke's MSS. Camb. MS. Add. 4478.

      See No. 230 below.

211. Catalogue of Pepys Ballads. Camb. MS. Add. 2650.

      See No. 194 above. FM seems first to have looked into
      the Pepys ballads during a visit to Cambridge in 1831.
      D, 2 Mar. 1831.

212. Catalogue of Roxburghe Ballads. Camb. Add. Vols. 2647-
      2649.

213. Catalogues of Ballads. Camb. MSS. 2642-2645.

214. Collections of Ballads: Lists, Bills, Letters, and Mem-
      oranda. Camb. Add. 2687.

      See No. 216 below.

215. Index to MSS. of Lydgate's Poetical Works. Camb. MS.
      4372.

216. List of Ballads. Camb. MS. Add. 2690.

217. List of Collections of Ballads. Camb. MS. Add. 2689.

218. List of Songs and Ballads sold by Birt. Camb. MS. Add.
      2691.

219. List of Songs and Ballads sold by Castnach. Camb. MS.
      Add. 2692, fol. i.

220. List of Songs and Ballads sold by Pitts. Camb. MS. 2692, fol. ii.

221. Memoranda on his Ballad Collections, etc. Camb. MS. Add. 2646.

222. Memoranda on MSS. Camb. MS. Add. 2651.

223. Memoranda on MSS. of Matthew Paris. Camb. MS. Add. 3019, fol. 76.

224. Memoranda on Oriental Palaeography. Camb. MS. Add. 2652.

225. Memoranda on Palaeography. Camb. MS. Add. 2693.

226. Memoranda on Writing and Language of Oriental Nations. Camb. MS. Add. 2653.

227. Notes, Misc. Camb. MS. Add. 2775.

228. Notes of MSS. in Cambridge College Libraries. Camb. MS. Add. 1027.

229. Transcript of Matthew Paris. Camb. MS. Add. 3019.

230. The Manuscripts in the Library of the Earl of Leicester at Holkham Hall, compiled by William Roscoe and corrected and improved by FM. MS. bound in 8 vols. deposited at Holkham Hall.

   Munby states (Bib. No. 289) that a fair copy was made for Lord Brougham, Vols. I and IV of which are in the library of the Grolier Club, New York. In 1932, Seymour de Ricci published an abstract of the Roscoe-Madden catalogue (Bib. No. 264). For FM's part in the compiling of the catalogue, see the biographical sketch (Part One), and especially Mrs. Graham's essay (Bib. No. 272).

231. *Caedmonis monachi Paraphrasis poetica Genesios ac praecipuarum sacrae paginae historiarum* ..., ed. Francis Junius, Amsterdam: C. Cunradi, 1655. Harv. 12413.36. 15*.

   J.J. Conybeare's copy with his autograph and notes and W.D. Conybeare's translation on the interleaving. Clubb (Bib. No. 261) identifies the collation notes, added in a very fine hand, as FM's.

232. *Laȝamons Brut*, 3 vols., ed. FM. Harv. 12414. 20.2*.
      (Bib. No. 82).

      FM's personal copy, with many corrections and other
      marginalia. He notes on the flyleaf that he had added
      in Vol. III four fragments of the later text, MS. Otho
      C. XIII., which did not come to light until after the
      pages of the book had been printed.

233. Glossaries to FM's editions of *Havelok* (Bib. No. 7),
      William and the Werwolf (Bib. No. 32), and *Syr Gawayne*
      (Bib. No. 70). Separately issued without title page in
      3 parts. Harv. 9287.6*.

      Contains FM's autograph and occasional notes, one of
      which states that only twelve copies were produced.

234. Copies of seven "Old English" metrical romances in FM's
      hand. Harv. MS. 27271.37*.

      The following romances are included: (1) Octavyane,
      (2) Isambrace, (3) Eglamore of Artasse, (4) Sir Degre-
      vants, (5) Sir Percyvell of Gales, (6) Romance of Ar-
      thur, from the Red Book of Bath, (7) Sir Degarre, cop-
      ied from a transcript made by David Laing from the
      Auchinleck MS.

235. MSS. and notices of MSS., XI-XIV cent. "Old English"
      poetry and prose. 5 parts. Harv. MS. Eng 526F.

      A large collection of miscellaneous material, amounting
      to about six hundred pages, largely in FM's hand. In-
      cluded are transcriptions from various MSS. of reli-
      gious poems and homilies, *Ancrene Riwle*, Bede's *De die
      judici*, a Psalterium cum glossa Saxonica, the poems of
      the Katherine Group, the *Moral Ode*, the *Proverbs of
      Alfred*, tracts, religious poems in Anglo-Norman, *The
      Owl and the Nightingale*, several Middle English lyrics,
      saints' lives, fabliaux, the Chronicle of Robert of
      Gloucester, and the like. In addition, there are
      drafts of material printed in FM's *Syr Gawayne* and of
      several items incorporated in Thomas Wright's *Reliquiae
      Antiquae*, as FM notes. A full analysis of some impor-
      tant MSS., in particular, the Vernon and Simon MSS.,
      is to be found in Part 5.

236. Collection of MS. notes and transcripts, extracts from
      periodicals, newspaper clippings, proofs, and other
      miscellanea. In 9 covers. Harv. MS. Eng 527 F.

FM's copies of short pieces illustrative of "old manners and customs," such as "The Dunmow Flitch of Ba-
con," "The Cock-Lane Ghost," "Hour Glasses," and "East-
er Eggs." A copy of *Index to the Additional Manuscripts
and some other Collections, Preserved in the British
Museum and acquired in the Years, 1783-1835*, London:
Printed by Order of the Trustees, 1849, with FM's annotations, proofs and copies of articles published by FM
in *Gent. Mag.*, copies of rejoinders to one of FM's reviews (Bib. No. 8), and other printed matter. Also included are FM's copies of "oaths or forms of swearing,
adjuration, and exclamations," of three Old French
lais, clippings on the subject of architecture, a
printed list of MSS. offered for sale by Count Libri,
and a MS. draft of the preface to Silvestre's *Universal
Palaeography* (Bib. No. 86).

237. Collections from the Arthurian romances relative to the
exploits of Syr Gawayne, made previous to the edition
of Syr Gawayne. Harv. MS. Eng 528 F.

Included here are a rough draft of part of the preface
to *Syr Gawayne* (Bib. No. 70), notes on the names of
swords and horses in Arthurian romance, notes on Owen's
Cambrian Biography, and a partial transcription of
Arthour and Merlin.

238. Translations of Old English grammars and a transcription of an Old English poem, etc. Harv. MS. Eng. 531
F.

Thwaites's Anglo-Saxon grammar, compiled by Edward
Thwaites from Hickes's *Linguarum vett. septentrionalium
Thesaurus* (Bib. No. 278) and translated into English by
FM. Dated "Batheaston, 1824." A short Anglo-Saxon
grammar, translated from the Latin of Aelfric, as
printed in Hickes and also Edward Lye's *Dictionarium
Saxonico et Gothico-Latinum*, by FM. Loose fragments
containing notes on Thomas Astle's *The Origin and Progress of Writing,* with copies of early English charac-
ters. "Poematis Dano-Saxonica Fragmentum," 1825.
Transcription of the poem *Judith*, from the *Beowulf* Ms.

239. Collection of correspondence and papers relative to the
"ant. Engl. romance of Havelok," 1827-42. Harv. MS.
Eng. 566 F.

Letters in response to queries concerning *Havelok* and
drafts of FM's correspondence on such subjects. Also

included are copies of Singer's *Remarks* (Bib. No. 304).
Professor Molbech's review of FM's *Havelok*, and a copy
of a review in the *Journal des Savans*. Included as
well are letters from Richard Garnett, 10 Apr. 1836,
and from William Thoms. The last-named correspondent
discusses the publication by the Camden Society of John
Robson's *Three Early English Metrical Romances* (Bib.
No. 303).

240. Memoranda from the written copy of both texts of the
      Wycliffite Bible (such portions as I myself have exam-
      ined), 4 vols. Harv. MS. Eng 573.

      Small notebooks recording MS. variants, in large part.

241. Thomas Tanner, *Bibliotheca Britannico-Hibernica sive
      de scriptoribus qui in Anglia, Scotia, et Hibernia ad
      saeculi XVII initium floruerunt*, ed. David Wilkins, 2
      vols., London: William Bowyer, 1748. Yale.

      Autograph notes by FM appear in the margins and on the
      interleaving.

III. *Special Collections and Miscellanea*

242. Collections relative to the County of Hampshire from
      inedited MSS., with a view toward a future history of
      that county. Bod. MSS. Top. Hants. e. 1–7 (*S.C.*,
      31140–31146).

243. Madden ballad collection. Camb. No shelf mark.

      As indicated in Bib. No. 164, FM collected more than
      27,000 ballads and songs over a period of many years,
      which Lady Madden assisted in arranging (D, 13 Mar.
      1861). He solicited Thackeray's help in searching for
      broadsides of the time of George I (D, 22 Aug. 1855).
      A number of ballads in this collection were published
      in a recent anthology (see Bib. No. 280).

244. Notes concerning Norfolk and Suffolk. Bod. Top. Nor-
      folk c. 3.

245. A collection of clippings, pictures, and the like illus-
      trating the history of the BM, 4 vols. BL C. 55 i. 1.

      See also Bib. No. 193.

246. Collections for a history of English ballads. Camb. MS.
      Add. 2688.

BIBLIOGRAPHY C

Works Concerned with Madden, the British Museum
and Nineteenth-Century Social History

[Works making significant use of FM's Diary or correspondence
are marked by an asterisk]

*247. Ackerman, Gretchen P., "John M. Kemble and Sir Fred-
       eric Madden: 'Conceit and too much Germanism'?"
       Forthcoming in *Essays on Early Anglo-Saxon Studies*,
       ed. Michael Murphy, to be published by G.K. Hall.

*248. Ackerman, Robert W., "Madden's Gawain Anthology,"
       *Medieval Studies in Honor of Lillian Herlands Horn-
       stein*, ed. Jess B. Bessinger and Robert R. Raymo (New
       York: New York University Press, 1976), 5-18.

*249. ————, "Sir Frederic Madden and Medieval Scholarship,"
       Neuphilologische Mitteilungen, LXXIII (1972), 1-14.

 250. Anonymous, Review of FM's *Laȝamons Brut*, *The Literary
       Gazette*, No. 1573 (13 Mar. 1847), 209-10.

 251. ————, Review of FM's *Laȝamons Brut*, *The Spectator*,
       No. 978 (27 Mar. 1847), 304-05.

 252. ————, Review of N.E.S.A. Hamilton's *An Inquiry* (Bib.
       No. 276), *The Critic*, XX (No. 504, 3 Mar. 1860), 262-
       65.

 253. ————, Obituary notice of Capt. William John Madden,
       died 2 May 1833, *Gent. Mag.*, new ser., CIII (May 1833),
       476-77.

 254. Barwick, G.F., *The Reading Room of the British Museum*,
       London: Ernest Benn, 1929.

*255. **Bell, Alan, "The Journal of Sir Frederic Madden, 1852,"**
       ***The Library*, 5th ser., XXIX (1974), 405-21.**

*256. Borrie, M.A.F., "Sir Frederic Madden," *The British Museum Society Bulletin*, No. 15 (Feb. 1974), 8-9.

257. Bronson, Bertrand, *Joseph Ritson, Scholar-at-Arms*, 2 vols., Berkeley: University of California Press, 1938.

258. Brook, G.L., and R.F. Leslie, eds., *Laʒamon: Brut*, Vol. I, *EETS*, CCL (1963); II, *EETS*, CCLXX (1978); III, forthcoming.

*259. Brown, C.K. Francis, "Sir Frederic Madden at Oxford," *Oxoniensia*, XXXV (1970), 34-52.

260. Casley, David, *A Catalogue of the Manuscripts of the King's Library: An Appendix to the Catalogue of the Cottonian Library, together with an Account of the Books Burnt or Damaged by a late Fire*, London: printed for the author, 1734.

*261. Clubb, Merrel D., "Junius, Marshall, Madden, Thorpe-- and Harvard," *Studies in Language and Literature in Honor of Margaret Schlauch*, ed. Mieczyslaw Brahmer, *et al.* (Warsaw: Scientific Publishers, 1966), 55-70.

262. Conybeare, J.J., *Illustrations of Anglo-Saxon Literature*, ed. W.D. Conybeare, London: Harding and Lepart, 1826.

263. Creevey, Thomas, *The Creevey Papers. A Selection from the Correspondence and Diaries of the late Thomas Creevey, M.P., ...*, ed. Herbert Maxwell, 2 vols., New York: Dutton, 1904.

264. de Ricci, Seymour, *Handlist of the MSS. in the Library of the Earl of Leicester at Holkham Hall*, Oxford: Oxford University Press, 1932.

265. Dickins, Bruce, "John Mitchell Kemble and Old English Scholarship," *Proceedings of the British Academy*, XXV (1939), 51-84.

266. Dodds, John W., *The Age of Paradox. A Biography of England, 1841-1851*, New York: Rinehart, 1952.

267. Edwards, A.S.G., "Sir Frederic Madden and George Hillier, and the Mostyn and Ellesmere Manuscripts," *The Book Collector*, XXVII (Summer 1978), 205-16.

268. Esdaile, Arundell, *The British Museum Library. A Short History and Survey*, London: George Allen and Unwin, 1946.

269. Evans, Joan, *A History of the Society of Antiquaries*, London: for the Society of Antiquaries, Oxford University Press, 1956.

270. Fristedt, Sven L., "The Wyclif Bible, Pt. I. The Principal Problems Connected with Forshall's and Madden's Edition," *Stockholm Studies in English*, IV (1953).

271. Garnett, Richard, "Antiquarian Club Books," *Quarterly Review*, LXXXII (1847-48), 325-42.

*272. Graham, J.E., "The Cataloguing of the Holkham Manuscripts," *Transactions of the Cambridge Bibliographical Society*, IV, Pt. ii (1965), 128-54.

273. Greville, Charles C., *The Greville Memoirs (Third Part). A Journal of the Reign of Queen Victoria from 1852 to 1860*, 2 vols., London: Longmans, Green, 1887.

274. Guest, Edwin, *A History of English Rhythms*, 2 vols., London: Pickering, 1838.

275. ———, Review of FM's *Laȝamons Brut*, *Gent. Mag.*, new ser., XXVIII (1 May 1848), 487-94.

276. Hamilton, N.E.S.A., *An Inquiry into the Genuineness of the Manuscript Corrections in Mr. J. Payne Collier's Annotated Folio, 1632; and of certain Shaksperian Documents likewise Published by Mr. Collier*, London: Bentley, 1860.

277. [Hanoverian Order], *A Translation of the Statutes of the Royal Hanoverian Guelphic Order with a List of English Knights*, ..., 3rd ed., corrected to 1836, London: Gardner, n.d.

278. Hickes, George, *Linguarum vett. septentrionalium Thesaurus grammatico-criticus et archaeologicus*, 2 vols., Oxford: Sheldonian Theatre, 1703-05.

*279. Hockey, Frederick, "Stolen Manuscripts: The Case of George Hillier and the British Museum," *Archives*, XIII (1977), 20-28.

280. Holloway, John, and Joan Black, eds., *Later English Broadside Ballads*, London: Routledge and Kegan Paul, 1977.

*281. Hunt, R.W., "A Dismembered Manuscript," *Bodleian Library Record*, VII (1966), 271-75.

282. Imlah, Albert H., *Lord Ellenborough. A Biography of Edward Law, Earl of Ellenborough, Governor General of India*, Cambridge: Harvard University Press, 1939.

283. K[emble], I[ohn] M[itchell], "On English Praeterites," *Philological Museum*, No. 5 (Feb. 1833), 373-88.

284. [Madden, Sir Frederic], obituary, *Annual Register*, new ser., 1873, p. 131.

285. ————, obituary, *Athenaeum*, No. 2368 (15 Mar. 1873), 344-45.

286. ————, obituary, *Royal Society of Literature of the United Kingdom, Annual Report*, IV (1873), 51-69.

287. Miller, Edward, *That Noble Cabinet. A History of the British Museum*, London: Andre Deutsch, 1973.

*288. ————, *Prince of Librarians: The Life and Times of Antonio Panizzi of the British Museum*, London: Andre Deutsch, 1967.

*289. Munby, A.N.L., *Connoisseurs and Medieval Miniatures, 1750-1850*, Oxford: Clarendon Press, 1972.

*290. ————, *The Catalogues of Manuscripts and Printed Books of Sir Thomas Phillipps*, Phillipps Studies No. 1, Cambridge: University Press, 1951.

291. ————, *The Family Affairs of Sir Thomas Phillipps*, Phillipps Studies No. 2, Cambridge: University Press, 1952.

*292. ————, *The Formation of the Phillipps Library up to the Year 1840*, Phillipps Studies No. 3, Cambridge: University Press, 1954.

*293. ————, *The Formation of the Phillipps Library from 1841 to 1872*, Phillipps Studies No. 4, Cambridge, University Press, 1956.

*294. ————, "The Earl and the Thief; Lord Ashburnham and
       Count Libri," *Harvard Library Bulletin*, XVII (1969),
       5-21.

*295. ————, "Sir Frederic Madden at Cambridge," *The Book
       Collector*, X (1961), 156-63.

296.   Oddie, E.M. [pseudonym of Elinor Mary O'Donoghue],
       Portrait of Ianthe, London: Jonathan Cape, 1935.

       Biography of Lady Jane Ellenborough.

297.   Payne, J., "The Anglo-Norman Words in Layamon's
       'Brut,'" *N&Q*, 4th ser., IV (10 July 1869), 26-27.

       A commentary on FM's failure to identify a number of
       words in the *Brut* as of Romance origin.

298.   Percy, Thomas, *Reliques of Ancient English Poetry:
       Consisting of Old Heroic Ballads, Songs, and Other
       Pieces of our Earlier Poets*, new ed., 3 vols., London:
       Henry Washbourne, 1847.

299.   ————, *Bishop Percy's Folio Manuscript*, ed. John W.
       Hales and Frederick W. Furnivall, 4 vols., London: N.
       Trübner, 1867-68. Vols. I-III subtitled *Ballads and
       Romances*; Vol. IV, *Loose and Humorous Songs*.

300.   Ponsonby, Arthur, *English Diaries, a Review of English
       Diaries from the Sixteenth to the Twentieth Centuries*,
       London: Methuen, 1923.

       FM's Diary is not treated in this work.

301.   Ritson, Joseph, ed., *Ancient English Metrical Roman-
       ceës* [*sic*], 2 vols., London: G. and V. Nicol, 1802.

302.   Robinson, Henry Crabb, *Diary, Reminiscences and Cor-
       respondence of Henry Crabb Robinson*, London: Macmillan,
       1869.

303.   Robson, John, ed., *Three Early English Metrical Ro-
       mances*, Camden Soc., XVIII (1842).

       In his preface, Robson acknowledges FM's indispensible
       help in preparing this edition.

304.   Singer, S.W., *Remarks on the Glossary to the Antient
       Metrical Romance of Havelok the Dane in a Letter to
       Francis Douce, Esq., F.A.S.*, London: Bentley, 1829.

305. Skeat, T.C., *The Catalogues of the Manuscript Collection in the British Museum*, Published by the Trustees of the British Museum, 1953.

306. Skeat, W.W., "English Grammars," *N&Q*, 7th ser., VI (1888), 121-22, 243-44, 302-03.

     Here Skeat published a list of grammars which he states was assembled by FM, and which he characterizes as "extremely perfect," and only comes down, in the main, to about 1840.

307. ———, ed., *The Lay of Havelok the Dane*, EETS, ES, IV (1868).

308. ———, ed., *The Romance of William of Palerne*, EETS, ES, I (1867).

309. Smith, Thomas, *Catalogus Librorum et manuscriptorum Bibliothecae Cottoniae*, Oxford: Sheldonian Theatre, 1696.

310. Tillotson, Kathleen, *Novels of the Eighteen-Forties*, London: Oxford University Press, 1956.

311. Toldberg, Helge, "Grundtvig og de engelske Antikvarer," *Orbis Litterarum*, V (1947), especially 283-311.

     A commentary on the exchange of letters between FM and C. Molbech in 1830 concerning N.F.S. Grundtvig, who translated *Beowulf* into English in 1820 and paid several visits to England.

312. Trevelyan, G. Otto, *The Life and Times of Lord Macaulay*, 2 vols., New York: Harpers, 1898.

313. Turner, Sharon, *The History of the Anglo-Saxons, Comprising the History of England from the Earliest Period to the Norman Conquest*, 4th ed., 2 vols., London: Longman, Hurst, Ross, Orme, and Brown, 1828.

314. Vaughan, Richard, *Matthew Paris*, Cambridge: University Press, 1958.

     Contains discussions of FM's edition of Matthew Paris's *Historia Minor*, as on 22 ff. and 205 ff.

315. Walpole, Horace, *The Works of Horatio Walpole, Earl of Orford*, 5 vols., London: G.G. and J. Robinson and J. Edwards, 1798.

FM attributed his early interest in antiquities to the account of the elder Walpole's treasures described in Vol. IV of this work. D, 18 Mar. 1842.

316. Warton, Thomas, *The History of English Poetry from the Close of the Eleventh to the Commencement of the Eighteenth Century*, 3 vols., London: J. Walter, *et al.*, 1774-81.

317. ———, *The History of English Poetry from the Close of the Eleventh Century to the Commencement of the Eighteenth Century*, new ed. [by Richard Price], 4 vols., London: Thomas Tegg, 1824.

318. Wiley, Raymond A., ed., *John Mitchell Kemble and Jakob Grimm. A Correspondence, 1832-1852*, Leiden: E.J. Brill, 1971.

*319. Winstanley, D.A., "Halliwell-Phillipps and Trinity College Library," *Library*, 5th ser., 2 (June 1947-Mar. 1948), 250-82.

320. Young, G.M., ed., *Early Victorian England, 1830-1865*, 2 vols., London: Oxford University Press, 1934.

321. ———, *Victorian England. Portrait of an Age*, New York: Doubleday, 1954.